w○rkingidentity

Unconventional Strategies for Reinventing Your Career

HERMINIA IBARRA

HARVARD BUSINESS SCHOOL PRESS

Boston, Massachusetts

Requests for permission to use or reproduce material from this book should be directed to permissions@hbsp.harvard.edu, or mailed to Permissions, Harvard Business School Publishing, 60 Harvard Way, Boston, Massachusetts 02163.

Library of Congress Cataloging-in-Publication Data
Ibarra, Herminia, 1961–
   Working identity : unconventional strategies for reinventing your career / Herminia Ibarra.
      p. cm.
Includes bibliographical references and index.
   ISBN 1-57851-778-8 (alk. paper)
   1. Career changes. 2. Career changes—Psychological aspects.
3. Self-actualization (Psychology) I. Title.
   HF5384 .I2 2003
   650.14—dc21

                                                    2002011665

Then indecision brings its own delays,
And days are lost lamenting o'er lost days.
Are you in earnest? Seize this very minute;
What you can do, or dream you can, begin it;
Boldness has genius, power and magic in it.

—*Johann Wolfgang von Goethe*

contents

preface

THE ANTICIPATION WAS PALPABLE at the venerable New England country club as men and women in sober business dress arrived one crisp evening in September. At the registration area, along with the usual name badges, they were given colored dots to put on their lapels. Each participant was asked to choose two colors of dots: one to match the industry he or she was currently working in (or had just left) and the other to represent the one he or she hoped to move into.

The club was holding a "structured networking" event for people looking to reinvent themselves, many of them managers downsized out of high-powered jobs. I had been invited to talk about using networks to change careers. People were footing a hefty attendance fee because they knew intuitively what I was there to tell them: that none of their existing contacts could help them reinvent themselves. That the networks we rely on in a stable job are rarely the ones that lead us to something new and different. The purpose of the event was to put into practice the famous "six degrees of separation" principle, whereby the fastest way to get to people we don't already know is through contacts as far away as possible from our daily routine.

The colored dots were designed to simplify the communication process, to replace the usual preliminaries, the "Who are you?"

"What do you do?" and "What are you looking for?" rituals we are forced to rehearse over and over again when we are seeking employment. The result was dazzling. The array of multicolored dots on each gray lapel gave the ballroom a partylike atmosphere. Few people had stuck to two colors. Their backgrounds defied categorization. So did their dreams for the future. They chuckled sheepishly as they explained the gumball machines on their chests. It was not one person who presented him- or herself to others that night. It was a rainbow of possibilities.

Preparing to Take the Leap

Like the people at the country club, we slowly awaken to a desire for change with some mixture of fear, excitement, apprehension, longing, self-doubt, anger, and dread. In this, we do not lack company.

"Am I doing what is right for me, and should I change direction?" is one of the most pressing questions in the midcareer professional's mind today. The numbers of people taking the leap to something completely different have risen significantly over the last two decades and continue to grow. But unlike the people at the country club, most of us face the chasm without the colored dots to signal where we have been and hope to go.

No matter how common it has become, no one has figured out how to avoid the turmoil of career change. Most people experience the transition to a new working life as a time of confusion, loss, insecurity, and uncertainty. And this uncertain period lasts much longer than anyone imagines at the outset. An Ivy League Rolodex doesn't help; even ample financial reserves and great family support do not make the emotions any easier to bear. Much more than transferring to a similar job in a new company or industry, or moving laterally into a different work function within a field we already know well, a true change of direction is always terrifying.

Finding a method to the madness won't make the ordeal effortless. But it can increase our chances of successful reinvention and, in doing so, of finding greater joy and fulfillment in our working lives. For even when career change looks like a random process, governed by factors outside our control—a life crisis that forces us to reprioritize, a job offer that lands in our lap when least expected—common and knowable patterns are at work. No career change materializes out of the blue. In the research for this book, I have discovered common patterns at the heart of even the most disparate of career changes, and a corresponding set of identifiable—if unconventional—strategies behind what can look like chance occurrences and disorderly behavior.

Changing Careers, Changing Selves

This book hinges on two disarmingly simple ideas. First, our working identity is not a hidden treasure waiting to be discovered at the very core of our inner being. Rather, it is made up of many possibilities: some tangible and concrete, defined by the things we do, the company we keep, and the stories we tell about our work and lives; others existing only in the realm of future potential and private dreams. Second, changing careers means changing our selves. Since we are many selves, changing is not a process of swapping one identity for another but rather a transition process in which we reconfigure the full set of possibilities. These simple ideas alter everything we take for granted about finding a new career. They ask us to devote the greater part of our time and energy to action rather than reflection, to doing instead of planning. Hence, the unconventional strategies.

Conventional wisdom tells us that the key to making a successful change lies in first *knowing*—with as much clarity and certainty as possible—what we really want to do and then using that knowledge to implement a sound strategy. Knowing, in theory, comes from self-reflection, in solitary introspection or with the help of standardized questionnaires and certified professionals. Once we have understood our temperament, needs, competencies, and core values, we can go out and find a job or organization that matches. Next come the familiar goal-setting, box-checking, and list-making exercises—the tried-and-true techniques for landing a job under normal circumstances. Planning is essential. The conventional approach cautions us against making a move before we are ready, before we know exactly where we are going.

But career change doesn't follow the conventional method. We learn who we are—in practice, not in theory—by testing reality, not by looking inside. We discover the true possibilities by *doing*—trying out new activities, reaching out to new groups, finding new role models, and reworking our story as we tell it to those around us. What we want clarifies with experience and validation from others along the way. We interpret and incorporate the new information, adding colors and contours, tinting and shading and shaping, as our choices help us create the portrait of who we are becoming. To launch ourselves anew, we need to get out of our heads. We need to *act*.

Before we can choose the colored dots that stand for future possibilities, we have to know what palettes (industries, professions, occupations) exist and what colors (specific jobs and role models) might best suit us among those within those palettes. This is not a theoretical exercise. We might say, "I'd like to start in warm tones," but before we settle on the right hue, we must explore a range of possibilities, testing them in the context of our daily lives. The same goes for changing careers. We need flesh-and-blood examples, concrete experiments. Working identity is above all a practice: a never-ending process of putting ourselves through a set of knowable steps that creates and reveals our possible selves.

Is This Book for You?

If your ears perk up when you hear about the lawyer who gave it all up to become a sea captain or the auditor who ditched her accounting firm to start her own toy company, and wonder how they did it, this book is for you. If you are curious about what is typical and what is rare among the cases you have seen—the person who yearns for change but remains stuck or the person who leaves it all for something completely different—you will also read these pages with interest.

This book tells the stories of thirty-nine people who changed careers. It analyzes their experiences through the lens of established psychological and behavioral theories. Based on the stories and extensive research in the social sciences, the book affirms the uncertainties of the career transition process and identifies its underlying principles. But the book does not offer a ten-point plan for better transitioning, because that is not the nature of the process. Instead, it lays out a straightforward framework that describes what is really involved and what makes the difference between staying stuck and moving on.

This book is *not* for everyone. It is not for the person just starting his or her working life nor for the person "downshifting" or easing his or her way out of a fully engaged career. It is for the midcareer professional who questions his or her career path after having made a long-term investment of time, energy, and education in that path. This desire for change might dovetail with hitting forty, as part of the famed midlife transition. But the midcareer population described here is much broader: It includes people who start a career young and return to school in their thirties as well as fifty-year-olds experiencing new degrees of freedom who seek a different way of spending the next fifteen working years. Whatever your age, this book is for you if you have experience to build on and the drive to make your next career a psychological and economic success. The book is also for you if someone close to you—your spouse, a close friend, respected colleague, favorite protégé, son, or daughter—is contemplating such a transition.

Most of us will work in an average of three different organizations and will navigate at least one major career shift in the course of our lives. Many of our friends, family, and professional associates will make similar changes. Knowing what twists might lie in the road ahead and what steps promote renewal won't reduce the great uncertainty about the ultimate destination. But it will increase our chances of getting started on a good path. What you can do, or dream you can, begin it.

Acknowledgments

I am grateful to many people for their contributions to this book.

The book would not have been written without the men and women who generously gave their time and shared their career transition experiences with me. While some of them are featured here, many—from whom I learned as much—are not. I deeply appreciate the lessons they taught me and I value the confidence they placed in me by allowing me to tell their stories.

I am particularly indebted to Kent Lineback for encouraging me to think of the book as a series of stories. If there was a turning point in the life of this book, it was my first discussion with him. Kent taught me structure and style, helping me to become a better storyteller and, in turn, a better writer.

Many friends and colleagues read early versions of my book proposal and chapters and listened to my ideas in seminars or conversations. Some of these people include Jeff Bradach, Fares Boulos, Martin Gargiulo, Pierre Hurstel, Rosabeth Moss Kanter, Bruce Kogut, John Kotter, Joe Santos, Barry Stein, Martine Van den Poel, and John Weeks. Jack Gabarro, Linda Hill, Nitin Nohria, and David Thomas watched over me from afar, helping me with this project in more ways than I can enumerate. I am grateful to Ed Schein and two anonymous reviewers for their careful and insightful feedback at a critical juncture.

I owe a tremendous intellectual debt to Bill Bridges, Hazel Markus, Ed Schein, and Karl Weick for their groundbreaking work on life transitions, possible selves, career anchors, and sensemaking, respectively. Their pioneering work in these areas provides the conceptual foundation upon which so many of my ideas are built.

The Harvard Business School supported this book in many ways. Teresa Amabile, my research director at Harvard, always believed in my "creative process." Dean Kim Clark gave me the gift of time, providing a semester that allowed me to write the first draft uninterrupted.

Many other colleagues at the Harvard Business School and INSEAD, my home away from home for most of this project, provided access and a forum for my ideas, including Chris Darwall at the California research office, the HBS club of France, and the INSEAD alumni association. At INSEAD, Deans Hubert Gatignon and, later, Landis Gabel, along with my OB group colleagues, also contributed by helping me to structure a time and space for writing.

It's hard to say when I started working on this project, but whenever that was, Barbara Rifkind was there, ready to listen and encourage me to think more broadly about my audience. Her role as champion, years before I was ready to write a book, made a big difference. Melinda Adams Merino, my editor at Harvard Business School Press, guided me through all the ups and downs of a first book with amazing patience and commitment. She managed to strike just the right balance of editorial advice and motivational encouragement, and I am grateful for that.

In her role as copy editor, Constance Hale made fine recommendations for clarity and style and was able to see thoughts as they were carried across chapters. Maiken Engsbye, my research assistant, helped coordinate the project and always gave prompt and responsive support.

Friends and family showered me with their support and interest, enduring long brainstorming sessions about my topic and title and the presence of my laptop everywhere I went.

Herminia Ibarra
Paris

one

reinventing yourself

W E LIKE TO THINK that the key to a successful career change is knowing what we want to do next and then using that knowledge to guide our actions. But change usually happens the other way around: Doing comes first, knowing second. Why? Because changing careers means redefining our *working identity*—how we see ourselves in our professional roles, what we convey about ourselves to others, and ultimately, how we live our working lives. Career transitions follow a first-act-and-then-think sequence because who we are and what we do are so tightly connected. The tight connection is the result of years of action; to change it, we must resort to the same methods.

Most of the time, our working identity changes so gradually and naturally that we don't even notice how much we have changed. But sometimes we hit a period when the desire for change imposes itself with great urgency. What do we do? We try to think out our dilemma. We try to swap our old, outdated roles for new, more alluring selves in one fell swoop. And we get stuck. Why? Because, as Richard Pascale observes in *Surfing the Edge of Chaos,*

"Adults are much more likely to act their way into a new way of thinking than to think their way into a new way of acting."[1] We rethink our selves in the same way: by gradually exposing ourselves to new worlds, relationships, and roles.

This book is a study of how people from all walks of professional life change careers. Looking close-up at what they really did—neither how they were supposed to do it nor how it appeared with hindsight—reveals two essential points that go against conventional wisdom. First, we are not one self but many selves. Consequently, we cannot simply trade in the old for a new working identity or upgrade to version 2.0; to reinvent ourselves, we must live through a period of transition in which we rethink and reconfigure a multitude of possibilities. Second, it is nearly impossible to think out how to reinvent ourselves, and, therefore, it is equally hard to execute in a planned and orderly way. A successful outcome hinges less on knowing one's inner, true self at the start than on starting a multistep process of envisioning and testing *possible futures*. No amount of self-reflection can substitute for the direct experience we need to evaluate alternatives according to criteria that change as we do.

These two essential points are the foundation for a set of unconventional strategies that transform what appears to be a mysterious, road-to-Damascus transition process into a learning-by-doing practice that any of us can adopt. We start this process by taking action.

Pierre: Psychiatrist Becomes Buddhist Monk

Pierre Gerard,[2] a thirty-eight-year-old best-selling French author and successful psychotherapist, remembers well the night he attended a dinner party in honor of a Tibetan lama. He and the lama, a European who ran a monastery in the French southwest, hit it off right away. Pierre had always been interested in Buddhism, and the lama was in turn interested in Pierre's professional specialty, how people mourn the loss of loved ones. The relationship that began that night would take Pierre in a completely unforeseen direction.

I'm a psychiatrist by training. Early in my career, I did a hospital internship in an AIDS unit, in the time before AZT. That meant learning how to live with the dying and learning how to accept death. During an internship, your afternoons are free, and I used the time to volunteer at an AIDS hotline. My next post was in a palliative care center where I worked for a doctor who helped change the course of my career. She didn't believe in the traditional medical detachment. She encouraged me to "go be with them and learn" and to take the diploma course in palliative care that she created.

In palliative care, you see all the worst pathologies. I was supposed to be learning the purely psychiatric side: the psychoses, the deliria. But those didn't interest me at all. I was interested in how the human spirit experiences physical pathology. Around that time, I was asked to create a support group for people in mourning. It all started coming together: the AIDS unit, the hotline, the palliative care work, and the support group. That led to my first book, on mourning. It sold so well that I have spent much of the last five years leading conferences on this topic. I love that: writing and training, communicating technical knowledge in simple words.

After medical school, Pierre set up a private practice. Classic psychotherapy never really interested him, and he much preferred working as part of a team, but private practice allowed him to make a good living after years as a poor medical student. He told himself that the psychotherapy practice was temporary and would be a good experience. "I felt a need to prove to myself that I could do it," he recalled, "and I believed I could help patients one-on-one." Private practice also gave Pierre the legitimacy to pursue further his passion—writing and speaking on how to help and survive the terminally ill—and afforded him an income that allowed him to devote time to volunteer in activities he found more meaningful. It all fit together.

When a doctor friend, also in palliative care, invited Pierre to the dinner he was hosting for the Tibetan lama, Pierre leapt at the chance. "I was thirteen, on vacation in Brittany and bored out of my mind, when I first picked up a book on Buddhism. It hasn't left me since. In fact, it was Buddhism that led me to medicine. But I saw it as a personal life-philosophy, not a calling."

"It sounds dumb when I tell it—I'm a very feet-on-the-ground person—but the second I met this man, there was an instant connection. Undeniably, there was something very strong there." The lama invited Pierre to visit the monastery, which also had a palliative care group. A short visit led to a collaborative project, a one-week seminar designed as a "confrontation" between traditional psychology and a Buddhist approach to mourning. Eighty people attended this first of what became an annual event. Pierre hit upon the idea for a future book, a Buddhist perspective on bereavement.

Connections started to form between me and the community: the monks, the laypeople, and the lama. There was no magic moment. Awareness came slowly. I can only describe what I felt as relief. I had already read all the books and had come to the end of what I could learn and practice on my own. So I went to the monastery more and more, at first every three months, then every month, then as often as possible.

In the meantime, a proposal for a palliative care center that Pierre spearheaded failed to obtain funding.

I killed myself on that project, putting it together financially, politically, and administratively. It didn't go through for political reasons. It was a big disappointment. And yet, I could see clearly what I found frustrating about that kind of role. I would have been the director of this center. When it fell apart, I sensed that even if it had gone through, it was no longer what I wanted.

So I went to the monastery, this time just for me, to replenish myself. I was exhausted physically and emotionally. One of the nuns offered me her house in the forest as a retreat. She said I could stay there as long as I liked. The thought of actually joining the community had never crossed my mind before. But one day I woke up in her little house in the woods and said to myself, "What if I were to do that?" I didn't want to be reactive, though. I was an expert on mourning, so I applied my own advice: I gave myself a year to mourn the failed project.

A year passed and the "what if" question kept echoing.

By this time I was convinced that my interest was not a reaction to any disaffection. I was in a long-term personal relationship that worked. I had a great reputation and was comfortable financially. But that wasn't enough. I projected myself into the future: more books, a bigger reputation, a nicer house. So what? None of that fulfilled my longing for spirituality.

Yet I resisted. Becoming a fully engaged Buddhist seemed crazy. Why give everything up? Why not just go there more often? At first, I only talked about it with the director of the center. He said it would be possible. Only months later did I consult a few other people. After that, I can't explain it. It is beyond the rational. It just slowly imposed itself as the obvious thing to do.

But it wasn't until a Caribbean vacation a few months later that Pierre realized the time had come to make a choice. "We were on a beautiful island and I kept going inside to practice. My partner finally said to me, 'Don't tell me you're thinking of entering the monastery.' I realized then and there that I had already made my decision."

In an initial, preparatory three-and-a-half-year period, no vows of chastity or poverty are required, and "helping work" such as Pierre's writing and speaking is encouraged. But after that, continuing as a monk entails a closed, seven-year retreat. "It is at the same time a radical change and not a change at all," Pierre concludes.

Buddhism is very much "in your head," like psychotherapy. It too, involves the analysis of human behavior and emotion. It's a coherent step, bringing together all the pieces that matter to me: teaching, belonging to a community of service, holding myself to an intellectual rigor, and developing the spiritual dimension I had been seeking in everything I did. I thank myself each day for having made such a sound decision.

Lucy: Tech Manager Becomes Independent Coach

Lucy Hartman, a forty-six-year-old information technologist, had long thought she wanted a high-powered career as an executive, even better to be part of a high-tech start-up that awarded its executives lots of stock options. As with Pierre, a chance encounter, with a consultant hired to help her company, gave her a glimpse of a possible new future.

When she dropped out of college at twenty, Lucy had no idea what she wanted to do. She landed in technology "by accident" and had the good fortune to work for a manager who encouraged her to take programming courses.

I just loved the problem solving and the precision that work required. I liked the sense of accomplishment I got from writing a program. Several years into it, though, I remember thinking to myself, "I hope I'm not doing this ten years from now." The glow had worn off. But I had no idea what to do otherwise, and the technology area offered such great prospects that it felt daunting to even consider a career in which I would have to start all over again.

Times were booming, and I had a number of opportunities at some exciting companies. I put in core systems for Basys just before they took it public, and for Microdevices. Next, I had a brief stint at a commercial bank, which was a mistake for me because it was way too big and bureaucratic. By that time, I was starting to feel frustrated with what I was doing. I went to a specialist in career renewal who gave me some assessment tests. She advised me to leverage what I was already doing into something new and different, so that I wouldn't have to start from scratch again. But nothing really came out of that. I just wasn't ready.

Then I went to Thomas Pink, a brokerage firm, where I had what I would describe as my career highs and lows. I implemented an extremely high-profile operating-system change that got me promoted to vice president. Technologically, I was the expert. But managerially, I was in way over my head. The people issues were beyond my understanding, let alone my having the skills to manage through them.

So we hired an organizational development consultant to advise us on how to build a solid management team and culture. I liked her so much that I hired her to coach me personally. The feedback she collected on me scared the living daylights out of me. I had imagined myself on a managerial career path, and I thought my people skills were among my core strengths. But she showed that they were not strong at all and that my coworkers perceived me as controlling. She worked with me for about seven or eight months, and the results were completely transformational. She engaged me with myself, arguing that I'd lost touch with who I was and what I wanted in my life. She thought I needed to figure that out rather than worry about how to climb the corporate ladder, which had been my obsession.

When I examined what I really wanted my life to be about, I concluded it was about connecting with people. Yet all my energy was going counter to that desire. I had this idea in my head that an executive at a company like Pink works seventy or more hours a week and doesn't really have time for anybody because there is all this stuff to do. I concluded that that was basically a crock, that I didn't have to work seventy hours a week to be successful. In fact, I started to realize that I might be happier and more successful if I invested more time in my colleagues at work and in my relationships outside work. My focus started to shift from tasks to relationships. My effectiveness improved as a result, but I also realized that I couldn't overcome some of the real barriers to change at Pink. I decided it was time for me to leave to pursue a career in a smaller company, where I could apply everything I had learned in the coaching. I went to work at ForumOne, a start-up, as a member of the executive team.

By this time, it was clear that I wanted to move on to something different. But I needed to build more confidence before taking a bigger chance on reinventing myself. So I decided to stay in the high-tech environment, which I knew well, but also to go back to school. I started a master's program in organizational development, thinking that at least it would make me a better leader and hoping it would be the impetus for a real makeover.

Three incidents marked a turning point. First, I attended a conference on organizational change that allowed me to hear the gurus and meet other people doing organizational development work. They had the tools to fix what I knew needed fixing in the high-tech world. I thought, "I want to do this. I don't know how I'm going to do it, but this is the community I want to be a part of."

Second, ForumOne was going through some acquisitions, and the restructuring meant my position was going to change. When I put my ego aside and looked at what I really wanted, I realized I did not want to run any of the new groups. What I really wanted to do was figure out how we were going to meld the two cultures in a sustainable way. But a number of our colleagues were stuck in a level of political jockeying that I didn't expect in such a small company, and much of my new job entailed "doing more with less." I wanted to spend all of my time helping people grow. When I was doing that, I loved it, but with so many other things competing for my time and energy, I was frustrated.

Third, one day my husband just asked me, "Are you happy? If you are, that's great," he said, "but you don't look happy. When I ask, 'How are you?' all you ever say is that you're tired. You leave the house every morning at 5:30 and you come home at 9 o'clock and you don't look happy." His question prompted me to reconsider what I was doing.

My original idea was to go work for a start-up. I figured that if I got lucky and the company went public, I'd have lots of money, and then I could afford to take a risk with a new career in which I might make very little for a few years. Then I started to ask, "What's really keeping me here?" When I looked at the gamble of staying for another year—when the stock might not be worth anything—it looked like I was gambling my happiness for more money. Still, I anguished about what to do for months, telling myself that it wasn't sane to quit a good job without knowing what you are going to do next.

The morning after my husband asked me that question, I had a sort of epiphany. I realized that I already had enough money to take a risk. What was holding me back was not financial security; it was plain fear that I might not be good at what I thought I'd be happy doing. I concluded that I might as well change now because I was dying to do something else and it would not get any easier with time. The next day—a year and a half ago—I quit.

I still didn't know exactly what form my new career would take. I said to myself, "I'll just finish my master's degree, try to get different types of work, and see what resonates." I started by calling everybody I knew. I went to different associations, contacted people who looked like they were doing similar things, and gradually started to build my practice.

My first client was ForumOne. The CEO asked me to help an executive in transition and to assess a new acquisition from an organizational perspective. That made it easier for me. It wasn't like I woke up on January 1 saying, "Oh my God, now what am I going to do?" I continued to work for them and found a couple of other clients. Believe it or not, my income the first year matched the previous year's salary. It wasn't all organizational development work at the start; some of the projects were straight management consulting. The mix gave me an opportunity to learn which new roles fit and which were too much like what I used to do.

By the time Lucy finished her master's degree and got certified as a professional coach, her organizational development practice included some of the best high-tech companies in the United States. "I love what I am doing," she concludes, "I am passionate about and fulfilled by my work in a way that I have never been before."

Different Paths, Common Plot

Pierre and Lucy each made a midcareer professional change. But, apart from that, their stories might not seem to have much in common.

Pierre's change—psychiatrist becomes Buddhist monk—is enormous by any standard. Few of us seek a transition as dramatic. In fact, Pierre's is by far the biggest "career change" described in this book. Lucy's change, in comparison, seems slight. Yes, she quit her firm. Yes, she is now doing a different kind of work, trading technical expertise for people and organizational know-how. And yes, it most certainly felt like a leap into the unknown to her. But she remains in the Silicon Valley high-tech world following the oft-seen path of the manager who takes his or her Rolodex and becomes an independent consultant at midcareer.

From a different vantage point, Pierre's change might seem less radical than Lucy's: At least for a period of three and a half years, he continued doing what he always did (writing, lecturing, and helping other people with their problems). A big community was waiting for him, ready to help, cushioning the leap. Lucy, on the other hand, was going it alone. She might have had a good network of fellow coaches and potential clients, but in freelance work, "You eat what you kill." Given her self-described attitudes about money and climbing the corporate ladder, not to mention the agony she suffered in deciding what to do, the kind of change she made might seem to take more courage.

Determining the magnitude of any work transition is highly subjective and hardly a relevant exercise. Who, apart from the person who has lived through it, can say whether the shift is big or small? For those of us who seek role models for changing careers, motives and trajectories are more pertinent points of comparison. In this regard, too, Pierre and Lucy are studies in contrast.

Pierre's story is about moving toward something that had grabbed him in his adolescence. Since the age of thirteen, his interest in Buddhism had grown deeper and stronger. He chose medicine as an expression of a calling that he continues to heed. But the scale and scope of what he would have to give up to pursue the calling as a monk posed a big dilemma for him. Though his case may seem extreme, variations on his quandary are common. Many of us feel a tug between well-paid, challenging, or stable jobs and the vocations we have practiced on the side, in some cases for the whole of our professional lives. Becoming a musician, a writer, an artist, a photographer, or a fashion designer at midcareer entails big personal sacrifices and typically dumbfounds the people around us, who fail to see why we don't simply keep our passions safely on the side.

Lucy, on the other hand, had been moving away for years from the technical career she fell into rather than chose. Knowing that something was missing but not being able to articulate what, she learned as much as she could from the exciting jobs and projects that came her way and hoped that each next step would clarify an end goal. At first, she wanted to climb the corporate ladder, moving from technology into management; next, she yearned to apply her new managerial skills in an entrepreneurial business; eventually, she realized she wanted to leave behind the relentless hours and the office politics. For those of us in Lucy's camp, who want change but lack a clear direction, the hardest part is finding an alternative to the path we are already on.

Like Lucy and Pierre, all of us approach the possibility of career change with different motivations, different degrees of clarity, different constraints, different stakes, and different resources. We move from different start points and end up at different destinations. But the differences stop here. In the middle, the vagaries of the transition process are strikingly similar.

Figuring out what to do with the next stage of one's professional life and how to begin it is a learning process with identifiable characteristics. Even when we don't have the answer or know where we are going, there is a knowable process that will lead us to the answer. As we will see throughout this book, even the most disparate career changes share a transition process, which figure 1-1 illustrates.

Identities in Transition

We like to think that we can leap directly from a desire for change to a single decision that will complete our *reinvention*. As a result, we remain naive about the long, essential testing period when our actions transform (or fail to transform) fuzzy, undefined possibilities into concrete choices we can evaluate. This transition phase is indispensable because we do not give up a career path in which we have invested so much of ourselves unless we have a good sense of the alternatives.

FIGURE 1 - 1

Identities in Transition

HOW THE REINVENTING PROCESS UNFOLDS

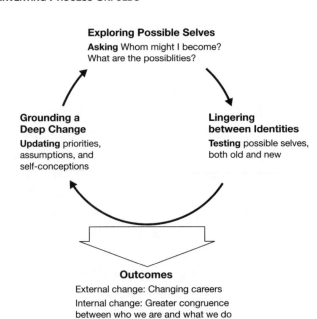

Exploring Possible Selves
Asking Whom might I become?
What are the possiblities?

Grounding a
Deep Change
Updating priorities,
assumptions, and
self-conceptions

Lingering
between Identities
Testing possible selves,
both old and new

Outcomes
External change: Changing careers
Internal change: Greater congruence
between who we are and what we do

Neither Lucy nor Pierre planned their way into their transitions, nor did they kick things off with a good dose of self-analysis. Instead, events in their lives and work led them to envision a new range of *possible selves*, the various images—both good and bad—of whom we might become that we all carry.[3] Some experiences presented new prospects, revealing alluring possibilities neither Pierre nor Lucy had considered before. Others helped them recognize outdated identities—roles that no longer really fit (e.g., a top manager), selves they thought they should become but were beginning to doubt (e.g., a center administrator). Still other occurrences raised the specter of their "feared selves," their worst-case scenarios of whom they might become if they chose to stay on the same old track (e.g., a harried, busy-round-the-clock executive). Change always takes much longer than we expect because to make room for the new, we have to get rid of some of the old selves we are still dragging around and, unconsciously, still invested in becoming.

Consider Pierre. Before the dinner party, Buddhist practice and values certainly formed part of his working identity; they had steered him to a medical career and helping work and guided many of his choices about how he invested his time. But "Buddhist monk" had never been a fantasized possible future, and even that night, he would never have dreamed of his impending career change.

So, how did his transition unfold? One step at a time. With each visit to the monastery, Pierre saw how monks lived, how they dressed, what they ate, what they did. Whatever vague (and possibly incorrect) image he held about Buddhist monks (e.g., they are always Asian) was gradually sharpened. By running workshops and by expanding his own Buddhist practice, he saw what it meant to be part of such a community. He was able to tangibly assess how much he liked it, where and how he fit in, what he brought to the table, how his competencies might be valued, and how his expertise might, in turn, be enriched by the Buddhist perspective. Pierre started to develop a working identity—still unformed, still untested—defined by his new activities and relationships at the monastery. In parallel, he continued his regular professional activities, including developing the palliative care center he was to direct.

Likewise, Lucy's encounter with the coach she grew to emulate led her to new activities and relationships in organizational development; these, in turn, shaped and changed her sense of the possibilities. At first, she imagined she was improving her management style and, therefore, working on her future identity as a senior executive. She left Pink to go to ForumOne in the hope of finding a fresh context for trying out some of the things she had learned from her coach. But the more she learned about organizational development, the more she was drawn to the idea of a people-focused, rather than a technology-focused, career. She enrolled in a master's program, going to school part-time and grabbing every chance she had to attend organizational development conferences or meet people in this new field.

Both Pierre and Lucy spent a good deal of time lingering *between identities*, oscillating between their old, outdated roles and the still distant possible selves they could make out on the horizon. After a while, however, both felt the strain of trying to live in two different worlds. Pierre lost more and more tolerance for the political nature of the medical establishment in which he operated as a psychiatrist. He came to resent time away from the monastery. And he started to feel torn between the helping work he loved and the hours he put in to pay the bills. Likewise, Lucy began to feel a tug between her old role as a top executive and an embryonic possible self that would allow her to focus all her energies on the people side of the business.

While new possible selves are still nascent, it is easy to fit them in on the side; but as they develop more fully, they crowd some of our older roles, provoking invidious comparisons. Outdated though they may be, our past working identities are not dislodged so easily. Their persistence confronts us with taken-for-granted priorities and assumptions about how the world works. These need to be reexamined before we can go any further. That's when the going gets rough. Once the change is under way but long before the transition is completed, different versions of our selves battle it out in a long and anguished middle period.[4]

For Lucy, her husband's question helped break the impasse. She realized that to shed her image of herself as a future, high-level executive with a brilliant corporate career, she also had to dismantle its underpinnings: her attitudes about money and risk, her self-perception as a "rational person" (one who doesn't leave a good job without the next one lined up), and her acceptance of long hours as par for the course. Progress from that moment forward required a deeper change than she originally anticipated; in the end, she had to reconsider not only the kind of work she wanted to do but also the kind of person she wanted to be and the sacrifices she was prepared to make to grow into that new self.

Pierre had long persuaded himself that he had an excellent portfolio of professional activities. He recognized that some were more rewarding than others, but he reasoned that his less fulfilling roles were enriching but not necessary. He had grown accustomed to segmenting his various selves—the team player who thrived on collegial interaction, the spiritual self who sought meaning in work, the intellectual interested in the psychological and philosophical foundations of human suffering, the educator who loved disseminating knowledge via his books and courses. On vacation, he realized he no longer wanted to compartmentalize. For Pierre, *deep change* meant establishing a greater coherence between what he did and who he was becoming.

Reinvention ripples through many layers of our lives. An outwardly radical change (psychiatrist to monk) can reflect a deeper continuity while what looks like an incremental move (executive to executive coach) can mask a profound change. What is important is not changing the work or organizational context but reworking outdated basic premises and decision rules that are still governing our professional lives. Pierre's professional goals have changed in favor of fulfillment rather than reputation. Lucy's work is no longer the central organizing principle in her life; her personal life is more balanced and money has become a secondary concern. Reinvention, as defined in this book, involves such shifts.

Identities in Practice

A view of human beings as defined by our "internal states"—our talents, goals, and preferences—is deeply ingrained in the Western world. This view is at the root of conventional approaches for making career decisions: If our "true identity" is inside, deep within ourselves, only introspection can lead to the right action steps and a better-fitting career.

Neither Lucy's nor Pierre's experience conforms to this model, nor do the other reinvention stories we examine here. Instead, like most people, Pierre and Lucy learned about themselves experientially, by doing rather than thinking. Certainly, reflecting on past experiences, future dreams, and current values or strengths is an essential and valuable step. But reflection best comes later, when we have some momentum and when there is something new to reflect on. Our old identities, even when they are out of whack with our core values and fundamental preferences, remain entrenched because they are anchored in our daily activities, strong relationships, and life stories. In the same way, identities change in practice, as we start doing new things (*crafting experiments*), interacting with different people (*shifting connections*), and reinterpreting our life stories through the lens of the emerging possibilities (*making sense*).

Long before they took the leap, Pierre and Lucy tried out their new roles on a limited, experimental scale. They made increasing investments of their time and energy rather than one momentous decision. Neither at the start imagined the magnitude of the changes ahead. Pierre's experiments consisted of spending time at the monastery, giving seminars, and developing his own spiritual practice. He began a book linking his interests in bereavement and Buddhism. Lucy hired a personal coach, attended seminars, and later went back to school for a master's while continuing her job as a manager. Even after leaving ForumOne, she experimented with consulting jobs to eliminate those too much like her old line of work.

Pierre and Lucy also shared the good fortune of having a guiding figure to help them over the chasm, and both enjoyed the encouragement of a new professional community. But these were not career counselors, outplacers, or headhunters, nor were they family and close friends. Instead, they found support in new acquaintances and peer groups. For Pierre, meeting a Tibetan lama who was, like he, a European, turned an abstract notion to a concrete reality embodied in a mentor figure. As he spent more and more of his time at the monastery, he found an intellectual and spiritual community he wanted to be part of. Lucy also found a role model in the organizational consultant whom she engaged at Pink. The consultant helped her see she was on the wrong track and pointed her to the community of organizational development professionals she immediately recognized she wanted to be part of.

All good stories hinge on turning points, dramatic moments when the clouds part and the truth is revealed. In this regard, too, Pierre and Lucy are typical. Both experienced events that triggered a realization that they were fed up with the old and ready to embrace something new. A project that Pierre had slaved on died a political death. Lucy's company was restructured and the political infighting heightened. Suddenly, both saw themselves in a future they no longer wanted.

Few working lives are untouched by organizational changes, internal management shuffles, office politics, and the stress, burnout, or disaffection that goes with the territory. But, these external triggers are rarely enough to propel a deeper change. The barrier, for both Pierre and Lucy, was a lingering hope that both old and new selves could happily coexist. On vacation, forced to make sense of the "non"sense of his actions, Pierre finally realized he had to choose. Lucy's husband's question, "Are you happy?" tipped her off to her rising malaise with her managerial role and the toll it was taking. For both, a small, symbolic moment, rather than an operatic event, jelled awareness that the time was ripe for change. Significantly, this personal turning point came late in the transition process, when both Pierre and Lucy were well along the way.

Pierre's and Lucy's stories are far from unique. Once we start questioning not only whether we are in the right job or organization but also what we thought we wanted in the future, the planned and methodical job search methods we have all been taught fail us. As summarized in figure 1-2, during times of identity in transition—when our possible selves are shifting wildly—the only way to create change is to put our possible identities into practice, working and crafting them until they are sufficiently grounded in experience to guide more decisive steps.

Overview of the Book

This book is about how people like Pierre and Lucy make their way to the next phases of their professional lives. It is divided into two parts that will flesh out the frameworks outlined in figures 1-1 and 1-2.

Part 1, Identity in Transition, describes the process of questioning and testing our working identities, eventually making more profound changes than we initially imagined. Chapter 2, Possible Selves, explains that although most of us would prefer to begin

FIGURE 1 - 2

Identities in Practice

ACTIONS THAT PROMOTE SUCCESSFUL CHANGE

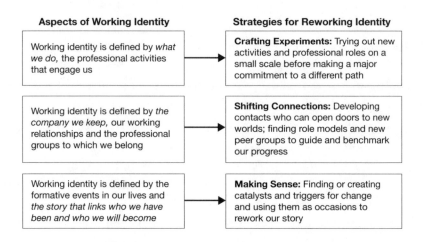

Aspects of Working Identity	Strategies for Reworking Identity
Working identity is defined by *what we do,* the professional activities that engage us	**Crafting Experiments:** Trying out new activities and professional roles on a small scale before making a major commitment to a different path
Working identity is defined by *the company we keep,* our working relationships and the professional groups to which we belong	**Shifting Connections:** Developing contacts who can open doors to new worlds; finding role models and new peer groups to guide and benchmark our progress
Working identity is defined by the formative events in our lives and *the story that links who we have been and who we will become*	**Making Sense:** Finding or creating catalysts and triggers for change and using them as occasions to rework our story

with a firm answer to the question, "Who do I really want to become?" the best way to start is by asking smaller, more testable questions, such as, "Which among my various possible selves should I start to explore now? How can I do that?" Chapter 3, Between Identities, describes the long, chaotic period of transition that begins when we start testing; during this time, identity remains undefined because we are not yet ready to give up our old roles, and alternative possibilities are still elusive. We are truly in-between. Chapter 4, Deep Change, shows how necessary this unpleasant time is, as our sense of identity shatters before it reconfigures.

Part 2, Identity in Practice, describes what actions throughout the transition period increase the likelihood of making a successful change. Chapter 5, Crafting Experiments, describes how we probe the future by transforming abstract possibilities into tangible projects we can evaluate. Chapter 6, Shifting Connections, shows how finding new mentors, role models, and professional groups eases our membership in new communities. And chapter 7, Making Sense, maps out how we rewrite the story of our lives.

The book concludes with chapter 8, Becoming Yourself, in which the unconventional strategies outlined in this book are summarized. It suggests ways to kick off the lifelong process of questioning and affirming the relationship between who we are and what we do. Making important career moves, and ultimately, life changes, requires us to live through long periods of uncertainty and doubt. We can learn much from the experiences of others to make these difficult passages easier to navigate.

part 1

identity in transition

two

possible selves

THE TYPICAL burned-out, stressed-out—or even merely disaffected—professional looking for change knows that he or she wants something new but doesn't (yet) know what. Those of us with a little more direction come equipped with a long list of career ideas—one that is usually well padded with sensible options that really do not appeal. Even when we have more precise notions of what's next, we tend to change our minds as we learn more about what they really entail. Bottom line, no matter where we start, our ideas for change change along the way, as we change. Where we end up often surprises us. For these reasons, as much as we would like to, we simply cannot plan and program our way into our reinvention.

Making a career change means rethinking our working identity. As Gary McCarthy's story illustrates, this is not a straightforward process of trading in an old, tired role for a new and improved one; nor can we always make progress along a straight and linear path. Trying very hard to go in one direction can lead us, circuitously, to another. So spending a lot of time at the start looking inside to find the "truth" that can guide a systematic search can be counterproductive (it may even be a defense against changing). Sometimes the best way to find oneself is to flirt with many possibilities.

Gary's Story

Everything hit Gary McCarthy all at once. After years of putting off the search for a more rewarding career, at age thirty-five the English business consultant got what he felt was a negative performance evaluation. His boss concluded—unfairly, thought Gary—that he had not pulled his weight on a key project. That was the last straw. It was one thing for Gary to decide to quit consulting; it was quite another for his company to tell him he was not up to par. That same week, Gary met Diana, the woman who would become his wife. The problem: He was already engaged to someone else.

"It was a snapping point," says Gary, remembering that time in his life.

The bad study and meeting Diana happened in close proximity and prompted a major rethink. I finally bucked up the courage to see MetaConsulting Group (MCG) for what it was—a job.

If I look back over my career, I have always responded to social pressure, what others thought was the right thing for me to do. After college, I worked at a prominent investment bank. I was working with someone I admired, but I found the work boring and repetitive. At the end of five years, I realized that running valuation models was not fundamentally what I wanted to be doing. The work is very, very cookie-cutter. I'd never seen how a company works. All I did was process numbers.

I wanted to do something different but was shocked to realize that people were already pigeonholing me. I tried to brainstorm with friends and family about what other things I might do. All the ideas that came back were a version of "Well, you could get a middle management job in a finance department of a company." Or, "You could become a trainee in a management program." That prompted me to go to business school in the U.S., which typically means "I don't like what I have been doing and I don't know what to do next, so I'll go to school for a couple of years and come up with a strategy."

I absolutely loved being in the States. I had always dreamed of living on the West Coast. But I ended up doing the "Gary cop-out" again, just as I did out of college. MCG offered me a green card and a perch in San Francisco for a couple of years while I figured out what I really wanted to do. So I headed out there for a new beginning.

I did not enjoy consulting at MCG for the same reasons I had not liked banking. I liked the problem solving but found the work repetitive, the tools constraining. Intellectually, I enjoyed analyzing companies, but I hated the treadmill. And you are always the paid adviser. I longed to manage the problem, not the client. I wanted ownership of the solution.

After two years, I took a three-month sabbatical. I was tired. I needed a break, having burned myself out on a couple of big projects. But I knew it was a signal that I was starting to go into an exploration phase again. I was still in the "I don't know what I want to do with my life" mode. I started looking at what I would call traditional transitions out of MCG. One idea was to explore alternative careers within MCG, in other offices. I spoke to the people in Hong Kong, where I'd spent my childhood, about helping them develop the MCG practice in Asia. At the same time, I started interviewing with companies like GE Capital, where I could combine my consulting and finance backgrounds. But it was obvious to me I didn't want to do any of those things.

The bad evaluation really knocked me out, because deep in my heart I knew that I wasn't as good at the job as I pretended to be. There was an element of truth to it. Yet it seemed unfair, in that it was delivered by a guy who had not spent any time understanding what was going on in the project. That combination of

*events was a catalyst: I was being told that I might fall off the lad-
der at MCG's instigation rather than my own instigation. I had to
recognize the fact that my heart wasn't in it and that I had been
going through the motions for some time.*

*I realized that until this time I had never said to myself,
"You'd better be damn sure when you wake up that you're doing
what you* want *to be doing as opposed to what you feel you
ought to be doing or what somebody else thinks you ought to be
doing." Within the space of three weeks, I told MCG I was leaving. I told them I wasn't even remotely sure what I was going to
do next, but I was going to take some time to think about it. I
broke off my engagement and left California. I up and went
home to the U.K.*

*Leaving California meant tearing up everything, both profes-
sionally and personally. It was shattering for those involved with
me, particularly my very staid British parents. "You're doing
what? You're giving up your job? You're breaking off your engagement? There's another woman?" But I had finally crossed a
bridge in my own mind, from the "insecure overachiever" mind-
set into an "I will decide what I do with my life" attitude.*

*It wasn't always easy, but it was an incredibly liberating
year. I stayed on the MCG outplacement list for the whole of that
year. I took up the offer of career counseling. It wasn't hugely
useful. They made me do two or three standard psychological
tests like the Myers-Briggs. There was the "OK, you need to start
thinking about what it is that you are looking for in your life"
approach and the "Are there jobs that you think you would actually enjoy being in, and do any of those make sense in the context of where you are today?" tack. Then it was, "By the way, if
you're going to go off to do something weird, we probably can't
help you very much." Based on that process, I divided my search
into "conformist" and "nonconformist" lines of investigation.*

*I felt that whatever happened, I was going to find something
I enjoyed and got excited about even if it was badly paid. Maybe
I got the idea from* What Color Is Your Parachute?[1] *I made a list
of people I admired and things I liked doing.*

It was a short list. There were two or three names on the "Choose someone you really want to work with" list: Richard Branson of Virgin, Charles Schwab, and, I think, the CEO of British Airways. Schwab was just launching the online brokerage, and that was exciting. British Airways was there because I've always had a great passion for the airline industry. Branson had always been a role model for me, almost a folk hero. So that represented combining the traditional path with an untraditional company.

The "nonconformist" path was to turn a passion into a living or to turn a personal interest into a small business. My passions were scuba diving and wine. Diana, who had by this time become my fiancée, shares my interest in wine. We looked at whether we could create a high-end wine tour business—the kind of thing in which we would arrange dinners with the owners of the chateaux. We'd be the tour leaders and live in a nice little house in rural France for a fraction of the price of anything in London, earning enough money to be cheerful and happy doing something we enjoy. We have friends who've done that. Diana and I went as far as drawing up a business plan for joining them.

But I felt that if I was going to go the alternative route— which meant a financial sacrifice—I was going to make sure I explored things I had always wanted to do. One was getting my scuba-diving-instructor qualifications. So I took two months off to go to Fort Lauderdale to diving-instructor school. I was surrounded by eighteen-year-olds, because that's the age when people typically become diving instructors. I was thirty-five at the time. I spent eight weeks going from just being an enthusiastic recreational diver to a certified instructor. I got as far as gathering sales particulars for two scuba diving operations—one in the Caribbean, the other in Hawaii—and trying to figure out if and how I could make them work.

I was starting to wonder if the diving business would lose its appeal after a couple of years, once I saw up close some of the mundane realities of owning a business like that. As my wife-to-be pointed out, I didn't want to spend the rest of my life scraping barnacles off boats. Looking back now, I think I might have done that for two years and then walked away, because it is a repetitive existence. I wouldn't have made any money. I would have discovered all the hardships and the boredom that creeps into life on a Caribbean island. I went to that edge and looked over and then came back again.

So when Diana said, "If you really want to do this, I'll come with you. But understand that moving to the Caribbean is not what I want to do. Can't you at least just look at a couple of other things that are a bit more normal?" I decided to take one more crack at what I would call a traditional career move.

When I got back, I spoke to some headhunters. I interviewed with GE Capital in London again, which confirmed that I would never like working there. I talked to two or three other companies. I looked at jobs in strategy, finance, anything with commercial responsibility. I called up the chief executive of Majestic Wine Warehouses off the cuff, because I liked their business model. That put me back into the "nonconformist" job search. I started calling a half-dozen people who I thought had neat businesses. My line was, "I'm really enthusiastic about what you're doing and would love to explore working with you." I was generally told that they would love to have me but couldn't afford me or that there wasn't a slot for someone with my skills at the moment. I called everyone I knew, figuring I could at least do some freelance work. I was having sporadic contact with Virgin, but nothing happened. I only had offers for traditional jobs, all of them standard career extensions for people coming out of consulting. I was about to go do a three-week project for Schwab in Birmingham, England, when out of the blue, the phone rang.

It was Virgin. I didn't know the guy personally, but he was part of the MCG network. I had called him a couple of times just to say that I was freelancing and he should call if anything came up. Literally, I had three days' notice. It was a project to explore establishing a credit card business. So I found myself catapulted into the new business group at Virgin. It was incredibly dynamic and chaotic, but for the first time in my life, I found myself enjoying getting up in the morning and going to work. And so I

spent the next twenty months here, technically as a freelancer, be-
fore I was offered a job managing capital portfolios.

The group I'm part of decides what businesses to start, grow,
or exit. It turned out that the tool set I had from investment
banking, mergers and acquisitions, and strategy consulting was
the ideal combination for this role. Would I have ended up just as
happy in any other setting where I could combine my skills? I
don't think so. What is different here is that I am working for a
person whom I've always admired, who's an extraordinary
leader and entrepreneur, and from whom I know I will learn a
lot. At the same time, I have ownership of my recommendations
and their results.

Models for Changing

Like Gary, most people embark on the process of changing careers
with some degree of turmoil and a lot of uncertainty about where
it all will lead. We can proceed from many different start points
and follow many different routes. But at the most fundamental
level, we all face two basic and interrelated questions: What to?
How to?

At the start, Gary lacked a clear idea of what to do next. So it
was impossible to devise a set of logical how-to steps. Like many
people trying to find a new direction, Gary mucked around instead, trying various things. He took a sabbatical to rest and get
some distance. He talked to headhunters, spent time with a career
psychologist, and availed himself of the MCG outplacement services. He talked to friends and family and bought best-selling books
on career change. He sought advice from top-quality professionals
and people who truly cared about him. But by his own account,
none of it was very useful.

Sure, he got started in the standard ways. He researched companies and industries that interested him, and he networked with a lot
of people to get leads and referrals. He made two lists of possibilities: his "conformist" and "nonconformist" lists. What happened

next, and what the books don't tell us, was a lot of trial and error. Gary tried to turn a passion or a hobby into a career; he and Diana wrote a business plan for a wine tour business. The financials were not great. He next considered his true fantasy career as a scuba instructor. He got his instructor certification and looked into the possible purchase of a dive operation. When he began to question whether the scuba operation would hold his interest long-term and his fiancée asked him to reconsider "more normal" possibilities, Gary went back to the list, which included both regular positions and design-your-own jobs working for role models. He went through several rounds of interviews with traditional companies and kept talking to headhunters. He thought about doing a three-week project for Schwab in central England. Finally, he took a job at Virgin as a freelancer.

Gary's seemingly random, circuitous method actually has an underlying logic. But this *test-and-learn* approach flies in the face of the more traditional method, the *plan-and-implement* model.

Planning and Implementing

The plan-and-implement model encapsulates the conventional wisdom of career counselors and business pages. A recent newspaper article summarizing "essential steps recommended by career counselors to get you started on your career change" indicates that the way to start is by developing "a clear picture of what you want."[2] The precursor to change in this typical—if flawed—model is self-asessesment: identifying "what skills you like to use, your areas of interest, your personality style, your values, and what's important to you."

"Executives who start down the wrong career path because of pressure from family or other forces and now feel dissatisfied may not know what type of work they'd find more satisfying," the argument continues. Understanding why we don't like what we are doing now is part of the equation; otherwise, we risk repeating bad choices. Self-assessment can also uncover and then help eliminate a mind-set that might be a source of resistance to change.

Once we have overcome the troublesome attitude within, we are ready to make change in the outside world. For the floundering professional, myriad self-help books and counseling specialists can offer assessment instruments to identify relevant personality types or interests and help answer the "Who am I?" question.

Once we are armed with more self-knowledge, the plan-and-implement method urges us to swing into action and proposes a thoughtful series of logical steps:

- Research career fields. ("Knowing your interests and most enjoyable skills allows you to begin matching them with professions and industries.")

- Develop at least two different tracks or lists of ideas. ("One might be a variation on what you're currently doing, while another might be a completely different profession than you're in now.")

- Go out into the market for a reality check. ("Begin researching your chosen field by reading about it and joining professional groups. Network with people in the same career and ask them what the day-to-day work is really like.")

- Home in on a career target and develop a strategy for getting there. ("If you can identify your long-range target, you can identify a critical pathway for getting there.")

While words of wisdom in a newspaper column can never come close to the counsel of a seasoned counselor, the article echoes the advice Gary actually received. What the article shares with more sophisticated renditions is a flawed premise of the plan-and-implement model: That the career-change process is best broken up into two manageable chunks, analysis and execution. We start by analyzing, and from that analysis emerges an "answer" that we can plan around. Then we implement the steps that will get us to that answer. Reflect, then act. Think, then do.[3]

Certainly the common practice of looking back over our careers and identifying what we liked and disliked, found satisfying and not satisfying, can be a useful tool for learning about ourselves.[4] And

Gary clearly benefited from the market research and list making. But the compartmentalized self-assessment and linear sequence implied by these popular approaches fail to take into account the most important aspect of the reinvention process: that we learn in iterative, multilayered ways. As we search, the new information we stumble across influences how we seek and absorb additional information. In this way, our working identity is continually shaped by the discovery of new alternatives. Through this rich, back-and-forth learning process, we arrive at the best career options, and only through it does our new identity acquire its full shape and definition.

Testing and Learning

Research on how adults learn shows that the logical sequence—reflect, then act; plan, then implement—is reversed in transformation processes like making a career change. Why? Because the kind of knowledge we need to make change in our lives is tacit, not textbook clear; it is implicit, not explicit; it consists of knowing-in-doing, not just knowing.[5] Such self-knowledge has a personal and situational quality; it comes from social interaction and involvement in a specific context and with specific people, not from solitary introspection or abstract information gleaned from theoretical, general-purpose personality profiles.[6] It can be acquired only *in the process of making change.*

The test-and-learn model for making change is based on theories suggesting that learning is circular, iterative: We take actions, one step at a time, and respond to the consequences of those actions such that an intelligible pattern eventually starts to form.[7] The self-knowledge needed is neither an "inner truth" nor an "input" that might light the way at the beginning of the process; rather, it is tangible information about ourselves relative to specific possibilities—information that accumulates and evolves throughout the entire learning process.

Of course, in any career change, deeper identity questions need to be resolved. Gary, for example, had to acknowledge that his insecurities had kept him from making his own career choices and that, as a result, his path was more the product of his parents' expectations than of his own interests and preferences. Although this was an important realization, it was not going to help him figure out how, and in what specific arena, he wanted to become his own person. A profound awareness of a problem or a growing dissatisfaction isn't enough: To make progress, Gary had to improve his ability to envision alternatives; to get a feel for himself in the contexts and situations he was considering; to test possible selves in situ, not just in his mind.

Management guru Henry Mintzberg once contrasted what he called "planning" and "crafting" strategies. When we think of planning, he argued, we think of a person who "sits in an office formulating orderly courses of action derived from a systematic analysis that precedes implementation." Crafting is completely different, involving "not so much thinking and reason as involvement, a feeling of intimacy and harmony with the materials at hand, developed through long experience and commitment. Formulation and implementation merge into a fluid process of learning through which creative strategies evolve."[8] The more unfamiliar the new possibilities, the more necessary it becomes to learn about them through direct involvement rather than planning. Because so many new ideas and bits of information surface once we get moving, spending too much time up front figuring out "the plan" wastes energy. As table 2-1 shows, the contrasting models for reinventing ourselves spring from a different set of assumptions and promise not only different means, but also different ends.

As we will see in the following section, the plan-and-implement sequence cannot lead us to a new working identity because its underlying view of the nature of identity and how it changes is flawed. A linear plan-then-implement sequence presupposes an existing, fully formed self that gets exchanged for a new and improved model, one that might have been known from the beginning. The test-and-learn sequence rejects the notion of a preexisting entity waiting to be discovered; it recognizes that a person and his or her environment shape each other in ways that can produce possibilities that did not reside in either at the start.[9]

TABLE 2 - 1

Contrasting Models of the Reinventing Process

	MODEL OF CHANGE	
	The Plan-and-Implement Model	**The Test-and-Learn Model**
Trigger	Pain, **problems,** or dissatisfaction in the present, growing stronger	Future **possibilities** growing clearer
Starting point	Interior, involving a change in **mind-set** (i.e., analyze, reflect)	Exterior, involving a change in **actions** (i.e., do)
Sequence	**Linear,** a process in which dissatisfaction with the status quo leads to setting a goal, from which flows an implementation plan	**Circular,** a process in which iterative rounds of action and reflection lead to updating goals and possibilities
End goal	**Fixed,** with the ideal of identifying the end goal as clearly as possible at the outset	**Changing,** with the ideal of improving our ability to formulate and test hypotheses about future possibilities along the way
Nature of the process	**Deductive,** with progress in stages, each building on the preceding step	**Inductive,** with progress by iteration with leaps of insight ("ahas")
Knowledge required	**Explicit,** an input to the process (e.g., what jobs exist, what skills we like to use, what areas interest us, what our personality is)	**Implicit,** continuously created throughout the process (e.g., what is feasible, what is appealing)

A Matter of Identities

No matter how unsatisfying our old jobs may have been, our desire to leave them makes us confront big questions about identity: who we are, who we thought we should be, who we hoped to become (or feared becoming), and what we risk losing in the process. This is not to say that "what we do" is tantamount to "who we are," but for most of us, work is an important source of personal meaning and social definition. Work activities and relationships are tightly woven into the fabric of our lives. In fact, work often provides the defining framework within which we set priorities and make decisions about other important facets of our lives. It is no wonder we feel so lost when that framework is in question. Or when, like Gary, we realize that we have not been the architects of that framework.

When the question "Who am I?" reasserts itself long after we thought we'd figured it all out, it is usually motivated, at least in part, by some form of what academics call "disconfirmation"—a tangible sense that our earlier ways of understanding ourselves and the world have failed us or that fundamental assumptions about who we are are no longer as sturdy or satisfying.[10] Gary's sense of never having grown up, for example, became a problem for him as he hit thirty-five and realized he had almost walked into the wrong marriage, in much the same way he had years earlier walked into the wrong career. What he had thought of as a provisional state of indecision now threatened to become a way of life. To top things off, his first-ever negative review threatened his belief in himself as a competent and promising professional. Gary's working identity had come undone.

How do we move forward and reinvent ourselves when our very selves have been so shaken? For starters, we must reframe the questions, abandoning the conventional career-advice queries—"Who am I?"—in favor of more open-ended alternatives—"Among the many possible selves that I might become, which is most intriguing to me now? Which is easiest to test?" Getting started depends on whether we are looking to find our one *true self* or whether, instead, we are trying to test and evaluate possible alternatives.

The Myth of the True Self

Career advice linked to personality testing is based on a psychological notion of working identity as defined by an "inner core" or a "true self." By early adulthood, the theory goes, we have formed a relatively stable personality structure, defined by our aptitudes, preferences, and values. These should form the starting point of any career search, because they determine what makes a good fit in a position and a work environment. Traditional approaches usually begin with a battery of tests to jump-start the process. Learning whether we are introverted or extroverted, whether we prefer to work in a structured and methodical environment or in chaos, helps us avoid jobs that will prove unsatisfying; knowing our true self helps us avoid a dead-end pursuit of fame, fortune, or social approval. In this context therefore, successful career change hinges on understanding what critical personal attributes hold the key to a good fit so that we can target jobs and organizations that match.

A related brand of career advice stems from adult-development theory, which holds that people develop through a series of phases, usually age-related.[11] Some of these theories claim that maturity—and progress—increases with each developmental stage; others suggest that as we age, we shift priorities, eventually attending to values and interests we had previously ignored. One argument goes that in early adulthood, we are all too often victims of other people's expectations. As we mature, however, we realize that many of our career choices were based on the desires of our parents, teachers, spouses, or unexamined (and often dysfunctional) institutional loyalties.[12] Development (that is, progress) means listening more to inner, rather than outer, voices in setting the priorities that inform our decisions. If we examine which family or other pressures might have led us down the wrong track, we can transcend pressures for social and organizational conformity in order to become "our own person."

The action steps recommended by true-self models are introspective steps: taking tests and interest inventories, for example, that uncover the personality traits that influence fit in a work context; engaging in therapeutic relationships with counselors, coaches, or psychologists, who can help diagnose the developmental underpinnings of the desire for change; or just taking time to reflect on what we have enjoyed and succeeded at in our past lives.[13]

Gary's counseling began with a battery of psychological tests aimed at giving him insight into his basic values and, by extension, helping him chart which work context and job might make a good fit. From those tests, he understood that he prefers to live his life and work in a spontaneous rather than methodical way. (No wonder that he did not love working within MCG's client-engagement structure.) The counseling reinforced his intuitive sense that he had fallen into a career simply because it was acceptable for someone of his national and family background. As he set out on his search, therefore, Gary looked for less structured and more creative environments than MCG (although not exclusively), and he made sure to make room to explore unconventional paths (although he still kept his "conformist" list).

Gary's experience shows that personality-based and developmental approaches have merit. Personality and maturity do affect professional satisfaction. But a static definition of identity—as an "inner truth" or "inevitable essence"—and the corollary change process stemming from the idea that we are (or should be) on a quest for a preexisting and knowable right answer are wrongheaded. Far more often than not, the true-self approach—there is a "right" career out there, and looking inward will give us the insight necessary to find it—often paralyzes us. If we don't know what "it" is, then we're reluctant to make *any* choices. We wait for the flash of blinding insight, while opportunities pass us by.

Even if we manage to get past the paralysis, the true-self approach can mislead us into thinking that the bulk of the work is up-front and diagnostic. After that, implementation is easy. Unfortunately, implementation consumes the bulk of our time and patience in career transition. What really happens in effective change is a necessarily "open-ended, tentative, exploratory, hypothetical, problematic, devious, changeable, and only partially unified" process.[14] The allocation of attention, time, and energy suggested by the true-self model is exactly backwards.

Myriad Possible Selves

A very different definition of working identity asserts that we are not one true self but many selves and that those identities exist not only in the past and present but also, and most importantly, in the future. Based on the work of Stanford cognitive psychologist Hazel Markus, this possible-selves model reveals that we all carry around, in our hearts and minds, a whole cast of characters, the selves we hope to become, think we should become, or even fear becoming in the future.[15] During a career transition, our possible selves spur us to find role models whom we'd like to become (and whom to avoid becoming) and help us to benchmark our progress toward those ideals. The more vivid these possible selves become, the more they motivate us to change. Why? Because we strive to become more and more like our ideals, and we scare ourselves out of becoming our most dreaded selves.

Let's return to Gary's experience. He did not make a clean start by ditching once and for all the "conformist" self he felt his family and social background had programmed him for. Instead he flirted with a whole range of possibilities, letting his own experience guide a circuitous set of steps that took him to Virgin and a new, more independent decision-maker self. As in a Darwinian natural selection process, he first increased the variety of possibilities, without even getting rid of the less desirable ones (he gave MCG and GE Capital a second and even a third try), before selecting some for closer exploration (the scuba diving) and finally settling on a new career in a fresh and compelling setting, working for someone he admired.

Gary's set of possible selves is typical in its number and range. It includes a "ditch it all and open a tour-guide business in the south of France with my wife" self; a socially respectable "MCG partner" self that his parents endorsed; a youthful and outdoorsy, "follow your passion" self who renounces convention and opens a scuba business; a "responsible spouse and future parent" self who wants to make good dual-career decisions; a "corporate drone at age fifty, full of regrets" self; an "apprentice" self who learns at the elbow of an admired entrepreneur; and a conservative "go to GE Capital where I can combine my backgrounds in banking and consulting" self.

Gary struggled with all these different possible selves competing for his attention. Some were fully formed while others lacked detail and contour. Some appealed to him more than others; some were imposed by ideas of what he ought to be. Some looked more feasible than others, given other facets of his life, such as his dual-career marriage. In his case, finding a new identity was not simply a matter of dropping one self in favor of another but a process of tinkering with a whole set of possibilities: imagining new ones, trying them on for size, elaborating on some, dropping others, getting rid of outdated images, coming to grips with the fact that some might languish. Only by testing do we learn what is really appealing and feasible—and, in the process, create our own opportunities.

Table 2-2 summarizes the differences between the true-self and possible-selves definitions of identity, illustrating how they correspond to the plan-and-implement and test-and-learn models discussed earlier. The plan-and-implement approach, rooted in a true-self definition of identity, treats an essential part of the picture as predetermined and immutable. It assumes that either our identity is given, our career options are given, or both. By contrast, the test-and-learn approach takes into account how our working identities and varied professional experiences change each other and how our early steps are critical in transforming possible selves into plausible realities.

TABLE 2 - 2

Contrasting Views of Working Identity

	Definition of Identity	Career Change Process
True-self model	One self: • Fully formed by adulthood • Resides inside, at the core of our being • Is rooted in the past, in family background and formative experiences	Plan-and-implement process: • Using introspection to find an inner truth that can help identify the desired end goal • Devising and implementing an action plan to get to that goal
Possible-selves model	Many selves: • Always changing, with some selves more developed or appealing than others • Reside in both our minds and our acts • Exist as images of the future	Test-and-learn process: • Shaping and revealing the self through testing • Learning from direct experience to recombine old and new skills, interests, and ways of thinking about oneself, and to create opportunities that correspond to that evolving self

Getting Started

How does one identify a set of possible selves? Charlotte Donald-son, a forty-six-year-old French-American money manager, made a list of possible directions two weeks after she left her broker job to devote time to making a career change. Twenty years earlier, Charlotte had fallen into a career in finance when she was just out of college. Dissatisfied with a job that no longer challenged her and a top brokerage house that failed to recognize her talents, she was now looking for a way out. When her office readied for a major downsizing, she volunteered to accept the severance package.

Before this exit door materialized, she had tried to fill the void in her professional life through outside activities—volunteer work, an interest in French food and wine, and contemporary art. She did organizing work for a U.S. nonprofit in Paris. She got involved with a professional women's network and, with the sponsorship of her brokerage firm, organized a series of seminars on women and investing. She took a night course on contemporary art. She did pro bono work for two of her clients, both wine specialists seeking to develop or expand their U.S. clientele. She hoped one or both might turn into a bigger project. But after a year of these small probes, Charlotte realized that none of them "were enough to get me going." She wanted something she could fully sink her teeth into.

After one summer vacation, Charlotte started making a list, albeit a more unstructured one than Gary's. She put everything on it, from concrete offers to vague interests:

1. Become a headhunter for finance executives at one of the top search firms. ("My sister's a headhunter. A few years ago, one of the top firms tried to recruit me. I went through the whole interview process with them. I know someone who makes a very good living with them.")

2. Do something in communications or investor relations. ("I'm a good public speaker. Everyone tells me I should be in communications. I know someone who founded her

own company in financial communications. I should try
to exploit all the financial things I've done.")

3. Combine private banking with art. ("I used to work with
   someone who went to Sotheby's to do investment advisory
   for art collectors; I love contemporary art. A couple of
   years ago, I was going to do a full-time course, but financial pressure kept me from taking the time off.")

4. Be a broker at another firm. ("I have an offer.")

5. Go back to school to study linguistics or history. ("I'm
   interested in political commentary, writing essays, doing
   book reviews. I always wanted to do a graduate degree.
   I'd like to explore writing.")

6. Do something related to food or wine and France, working as a liaison to the United States. ("I have a lot of interests related to food. We have a country house, and I've
   gotten to know some of the local chefs and products.
   I might be able to exploit my American side.")

7. Do something else that exploits my bicultural, bilingual
   background.

8. Take a relatively unknown luxury brand international.
   ("I'm interested in niche, upscale products related to the
   home, like porcelain or crystal. When I worked in Asia,
   I considered starting an export business.")

The list is telling. It outlines Charlotte's possible selves. Her
reasonable, practical self, who thinks being a headhunter is a good,
safe compromise. Her old role projected into the future, via the do-
the-same-thing-at-another-firm offers (she is not yet at the stage
where she can take that off the list). An old, fantasy self, marrying
art and finance, whom she had yearned to explore a few years before. Today's fantasy self, who goes back to school and tries her
hand at writing. The selves seen by others who know her well and
think she should exploit her presence and communication skills.

Her list looks like countless others. A possible-selves list always has a favorite (and it is always near the bottom of the list, as

if we were fearful of even exposing it). The list often starts with what gets framed as the "reasonable option," one that exploits the past but in a new context or job. The tone used to describe this path betrays its lack of appeal. The list typically has something on it we really do not want to do. Sometimes it has role models, people whom we would like to be like. More often than not, it also has things we really have no intention of actually exploring but that add color to the list or are thrown in to round things out.

What do we do with such a list? We start to act, in order to find out what to cross off and what to explore. So many of us can say, "But I'm interested in lots of things. That's my problem." Once the list is done, the hard part begins: bringing some of those possible selves into the world, to evaluate them more closely. In Charlotte's view, a danger lurked in moving too quickly. Remembering an earlier—and misguided—career move she made because an offer landed in her lap, Charlotte now insisted on taking the time to figure out what she really wanted. She resisted the urge to throw herself full-tilt into the job market right away. But, a great danger lies in devoting months—worse yet, years—of self-reflection before taking a first step. Instinctively, Charlotte knew to look for a project to tide her over.

> I need something to give me some structure while I figure this out. I'm going to take over a fund-raising campaign for a nonprofit I'm involved with. That will keep me busy yet leave me time to explore. There has to be a grant out there for someone to study the history of Burgundy cooking. I'd like to develop a project, something doable, with a start and finish, so I can test the "Do I like to write? Can I write something that is convincing?" idea. Something to give me a good excuse for taking time off, so when someone at a party asks me what I do, I can say I'm on a grant.

Still, the hard part was just beginning. "I've been surprised by the violence of my feelings," Charlotte observed after her vacation.

It's only been two weeks. I see myself as someone who thinks out-side the box, so I thought I'd let my imaginative juices run. But I came back after summer vacation and thought, "Oh my God, it's September. I don't have a place to go or a plan." My husband would like to be more supportive. But he can't. His view is, "Where's your business plan?" It makes me feel fragile. Not worthless, but unsure about where I fit in. It makes me ask, "Am I too old? Is this as far as I'm going to go?" I feel like I'm sup-posed to be more together.

So many of us, like Gary, have fantasies about whom we'd like to be but, unlike him, we never test them. Like Charlotte, we make the list, only to become confused and overwhelmed by the vast range of possibilities. What happens once the list is done, however, is all-determining: That is when we need to move quickly to bring at least one of the items on the list into the world. Giving form and order to our possible selves, making them tangible, bringing them into the world, is hard work—both cognitively and emotionally. This trying middle period between old and new, when we are re-constructing the set of possibilities of whom we might become, is the subject of the next chapter.

three

between identities

T HE REINVENTING PROCESS is rarely quick or easy, even for the veteran job-hopper. Emotionally, it is hard to let go of a career in which we have invested much time, training, and hard work. Letting go is even harder when the alternatives remain fuzzy. And yet there's no avoiding this agonizing period between old and new careers: A transition can begin years before a concrete alternative materializes, as we start creating and testing possible selves.

This chapter describes the long and difficult middle period when our identities are in flux. In this transitional state, as June Prescott's story shows, we oscillate between holding on to the past and embracing the future. We move forward without clearly defined destinations, and we gather the courage to leave behind activities and relationships that have been central to how we define ourselves. The *in-between period* is the crucible in which we bring our possible selves tentatively into the world. Unpleasant as it may be, we short-circuit it at our own peril.

June's Story

One night, a year and a half into her efforts to change careers, June Prescott had a dream. "I felt myself falling, falling, falling down. I am a tower and I turn round and round, tumbling down, till I hit bottom. There I discover I am still alive and relatively unhurt, still a tower, recovered from my fall."

The dream was not hard for June to interpret. It closely paralleled what she felt in her waking hours. She was in the last months of a Spanish literature professorship, a career she had passionately entered after college but grown out of. Her plans for a second career in finance had yet to pan out despite persistent efforts. What next? She simply did not know.

A native New Yorker, June had started thinking about making a new career about two and a half years before, when she was forty. It was a time of many changes, both personal and professional. During a one-year sabbatical in New York, she married; had her first child; and started to flirt with the idea of moving out of academia, stealing some time earmarked for a book project to dabble in real estate. Reentering her academic department after her first daughter was born had been brutal. She had always been the bright star of her department, the chairman's protégé. Now as her next review approached, she realized she had not prepared herself for tenure and did not want to stay at the university. Her old mentor was no longer the department chairman. The new head, his bitter rival, piled responsibilities on, leaving her precious little time for writing. The petty politics that she had always found annoying but amusing became intolerable, even more so after her second daughter was born. June was also the family's primary breadwinner, and the reality of putting her girls through school on a humanities salary had sunk in.

The stock market became her antidote to anxiety about the future. Her broker, a woman who recognized June's nose for the markets, encouraged her to play with part of her nest egg. June's choices were inspired; she made good returns; and she discovered that she loved researching stocks and companies, reading everything she could on the topic. Instead of working on her book, she found herself glued to CNBC, reading the investment chat boards, devouring *Barron's*, swept away on the thrill of the bull market.

One day a friend took her to a trading floor, and the experience sparked a desire to learn more about the capital markets. This excitement echoed that of an earlier brief encounter:

> *I visited the Upper-East-Side home of a woman who made several hundred thousand dollars a month doing trades from her home. She owned one of those beautiful old brownstones, a block from where I lived on the corner of Fifth Avenue. The building had five floors, and on the fourth one was a large room, perfectly empty but for five computers sitting in a row, dedicated to trading in the markets. I was going to ask her if I could come over and watch her trade one day, but I didn't have the nerve.*

It began to dawn on June that she might turn her new passion into a career, possibly linking her Spanish expertise and contacts to something in finance. But she did not even know what kinds of jobs existed. Personal contacts led to a couple of informational interviews. A former Morgan Stanley employee suggested she look into researching Spanish and Portuguese companies or providing private client services for wealthy Iberians. Next, June started to frequent the career services center on campus to find out about companies that recruited there. When they came to hire undergraduates, she managed to get a foot in the door. Personable and resourceful, June ended up interviewing with the likes of Goldman Sachs and Lehman Brothers.

By trial and error, she learned not just the nature of investment banking but also the nuances of interviews and the protocols of cover letters in the business world. But nothing came of her efforts. Her age and background made her a round peg trying to fit in a square hole. In college, June had majored in literature, and she had gone on to collect an impressive number of graduate degrees, all in the humanities. She was a specialist in the Spanish Renaissance.

But she had never worked outside a university setting. Potential employers were drawn by her personality and drive, and she was attracted by the prospect of working with smart people and getting good training. But after every interview, an offer failed to materialize. The companies did not know what to do with her:

> Both my father and sister explained to me with passion, and a few milligrams of reason, that no one was going to give me an entry-level position. I was a professor with a Ph.D., and they knew that I would never be satisfied being a lackey for someone else. I would learn quickly and leave the position as soon as possible, probably to go to another firm. My good intentions notwithstanding, they knew I would not like it and I wouldn't stick it out. Lehman told me they were considering me for a position, but they didn't know which, because they would not offer me an entry-level job.

After months of variations on the same theme, June realized that making this kind of transition would be no easy matter. She had two toddlers and a demanding job. Getting an M.B.A. was out of the question since she could not afford it. Luckily, that period had been a good one for the stock market: In a few months' time, June made the equivalent of half her annual salary. Cashing in the returns, she funded herself a semester without teaching.

During the spring "sabbatical," she designed a new literature course and made plans to publish a reader on the topic. She worked in fits and starts on a book about Renaissance literature, the one she did not finish in New York. She flirted again with a longtime backup plan, taking an administrative position at the university and transitioning into a "quiet life." But again, June found herself drawn to the capital markets and devoted more and more of her time to learning about companies and investments. As summer approached with no reward in sight for all her efforts, she called a moratorium to enjoy time at the beach with her family.

With renewed energy in the fall, June signed up to audit two M.B.A. courses, macroeconomics and financial instruments and contracts, at her university's business school. She also enrolled in a Portuguese language class. She taught two literature courses, advising freshmen into the night, then rushed home to prepare her problem sets for business school. The M.B.A course project teams were the hardest. It seemed that everyone but her had some expertise to contribute. Her team members did not take her seriously: She had never been an investment banker, never taken an accounting course. She had to take extra classes on Excel and PowerPoint just to keep up.

The real action, she learned, happened outside class, in the recruiting and networking events offered by the business school. So June attended all the presentations given by the investment banks—DLJ, Chase, Merrill, Citibank—even when that meant rescheduling the courses she taught as a professor. As an outsider to the business school, getting in took some stealth tactics. The pace was relentless. Just the cycle of updating her résumé, writing cover letters, and sending follow-up thank-you notes seemed like a full-time job. She wondered how she had managed to get interviews the year before, in her blissful ignorance of how things really worked.

June also pursued another idea: finding a person she admired and convincing him to take her on as an apprentice. One candidate was James Cramer, a financial pundit who wrote a column for the *Wall Street Journal*. June admired his wit and writing style as much as his insights into the markets. By e-mail, she told him how much she enjoyed his writing and asked for a meeting. Cramer agreed. He advised her to keep a journal to track her impressions and experiences. A relationship began in which he challenged and guided her.

June found other kindred spirits, including her macroeconomics teaching assistant, who had a joint divinity and economics Ph.D. When an old college friend in the Slavic studies department started a search for a consulting job, the two pooled resources, editing each other's résumés and sharing their anxieties.

Eventually, business school interview mania hit, and June broadened her search.

At the last minute, I decided to apply for the consulting jobs. The McKinsey application required an essay from Ph.D.'s. I really enjoyed it. The guy I met from Monitor Consulting was likable and smart. I went to another consulting firm presentation, where I met a brilliant woman physicist. She is one of the most amazing women I've ever met. She interviewed me and then offered to help prepare me for the case interviews. Though I don't believe consulting is my destiny, because of the lifestyle it requires, it seemed like extremely interesting and challenging work.

The appeal of consulting, however, lessened upon closer examination. "These consulting firms remind me of true psychoanalysts who believe that there is only one way to understand and change human behavior," she wrote.

I spent a couple of hours on the Mercer site. You would think you were climbing Mount Everest with your "tool kit" or doing Outward Bound with a bunch of Olympic champions. It's less complex to apply for a Rhodes scholarship. I did the interactive case online. My girls were screaming and crying, so I used only nine minutes, the mother's version of the thirty they give you. I got the recommendation right, though I asked too many specific questions at the beginning and I market-sized wrong.

She stepped up the Wall Street search.

Lehman has taken a new turn; apparently they might need someone to go to Europe. They called yesterday for another copy of my résumé, which has already changed twice more this week. My next career will be as a résumé writer. I just applied for another job at Bank of America Securities. I went to JP Morgan's presentation last night. It was very short and to the point. No nonsense. Nice people. I talked to the presenter, a managing director, afterward. He has an M.A. from Yale in philosophy and theology, from the divinity school! Then he got his J.D. at the law school and has worked at JP since. I gave him my résumé.

With each round of interviewing, June saw the links between old and new more clearly: "At first I wondered what I would do with my knowledge of literature. It seemed like such a waste. But then I realized that what I have always wanted is a job that keeps me constantly interested and always learning new things." With each round, she also met more and more people who, like she, had "unconventional backgrounds," or who impressed her as role models for whom she'd like to become: "I met an extraordinary woman—super smart and super nice—in fixed-income research, who graduated from my alma mater around the same time I did. She promised to call when she got back from her honeymoon." As she improved her knowledge of the rules of the game, she even began to improvise possibilities. She interviewed with DLJ, deciding on the spot to tell them she wanted to be a researcher on the entertainment industry.

June's stockbroker, who worked for Taylor Roberts, a rapidly growing U.S. brokerage house, encouraged her to apply there. The training offered was thorough and the you-run-your-own-business setup amenable to balancing family life. It seemed a good way to cut her teeth. But she stuck to her strategy of "going for the top names," figuring that starting at one of the most prominent companies would offer the best learning opportunities and create the most flexible platform for an unknown future.

Teaching literature was still fun. But June's connection to her colleagues had deteriorated. She had grown to dislike many of the people she worked with. There was not a single one among them whom she wanted to be like. Friends who had left the department advised her to move, certain that she would be happier pursuing her academic career elsewhere. Still, she anguished.

I was loving teaching my classes. I had great students. But my literature colleagues seemed nervous, hostile, and awkward. I felt extremely distant from everyone. In fact, I was feeling a total disconnect from the department. One weekend I went through my files and found four unfinished articles, part of a second book—eighty pages—and all the stuff from the first book I was working

*on. It stunned me to think that if I finished that stuff, I would
have tenure for life somewhere. I spent a good chunk of that
weekend rewriting one of the articles, on Renaissance utopianism
and the exploration of the Americas, as a writing sample for a job
application. I enjoyed it tremendously and decided to send it out
to a good journal when I finished it.*

A turning point came as the deadline for June's contract renewal as a faculty member loomed. Looking back, she realized
that at each time she had had a choice in how to spend her time,
she had invested in other avenues; looking forward, the prospect
of a tenured post had lost its appeal. Not wanting to continue pre-
tending, she announced that she would not come up for review.
Effectively, this gave her six months, until her university contract
expired, to find a new job. "I thought it was going to feel like a divorce, a huge loss," she recounts, "but it didn't. I loved my business courses and the project groups. It's a lot easier when you feel
emotionally involved in something else."

A good job, defined in the humanities as a permanent tenure-
track position in a reasonably sized city, came up in June's subfield.
Her mentor could barely contain his disbelief that she did not put
in an application. Her heart was just not in it. Yet the idea of giving up teaching, for which she believed she had a true calling, was
tough. Despite a more-than-full schedule, she volunteered her time
to an ambitious program for inner-city high-school teachers. Her
husband urged her to consider again stepping off the tenure track
and moving into a secure university administration job. But, as
scary as it seemed, deep down June relished the idea of finally cut-
ting her ties to the university where she had gone to college, returned for her Ph.D., and now worked as faculty.

As the holiday season approached, the euphoria of new possibilities was dampened by the paucity of job prospects. June always
knew her age and background made her a tough sell; now she was
coming to the conclusion that being a mother might also work
against her: "Once two of my more promising prospects learned I
had two children, it was over. Anything that indicated I might not

give 100 percent meant the end of the story." She began to reconsider alternatives to an M.B.A., since her lack of such a credential seemed to be disadvantaging her. It was a confusing time; all and nothing seemed possible.

"It is Sunday and I don't know where to begin working," June mused at that juncture.

Maybe when I finish this coffee, all will clarify. For now, it's up for grabs: Shall I clean the house; buy food for the family; read El Burlador de Sevilla, *which I assigned to my students for class tomorrow; go to the business school to search the alumni database for names of people working at the firms I've applied to; learn more Excel; or look for information about alternatives to an M.B.A. program? My husband thinks I should start talking to people about staying here in some capacity or another. I, of course, want a new career, a new life, independence, new knowledge, excitement, passion, and challenges. In the meantime, I continue to learn and I continue to make mistakes. It is like living inside a hurricane.*

In the Middle

It's always ugly in the middle.

At the root of *transition* is "transit," a voyage from one place to another. As in any voyage, there is a departure, a disorienting time of travel and, finally, a destination. Transitions guru William Bridges calls the time between endings and new beginnings the "neutral zone," a "neither here nor there" psychological space where identities are in flux and people feel they have lost the ground beneath their feet.[1] As June's story illustrates, this in-between period is not a literal space between one job and the next but a psychological zone in which we are truly between selves, with one foot still firmly planted in the old world and the other making tentative steps toward an as-yet undefined new world. Whether a person is working two jobs at once, finishing a lame-duck period, in outplacement, or taking an extended time to reflect on what comes next, the experience that June described as "living inside a hurricane" is common. It is a time rife with anticipation, confusion, fear, and all sorts of other mixed feelings.

To be in transit is to be in the process of leaving one thing, without having fully left it, and at the same time entering something else, without being fully a part of it.[2] It is a gestation period of provisional, tentative identity when many different selves are possible and none are obvious. The psychology of this in-between period has been described as ambivalence: We oscillate between "holding on" and "letting go," between our desire to rigidly clutch the past and the impulse to rush exuberantly into the future.[3] Over a period of months or even years, we move back and forth between these poles as we explore new roles and possibilities. Rather than being a sign of one's lack of readiness, this moving back and forth is in fact the key to successful transitioning. It is how we stave off premature closure until we have fully explored alternatives.

Becoming an "Ex"

People who undergo extreme identity transitions (leaving a religious order, say, or undergoing sex-change surgery) and people who make more mundane career and life changes, such as leaving the practice of medicine or getting divorced, share common experiences, according to one sociological study.[4] Like June, who was leaving a career for which she had studied so many years, people in the process of "becoming an ex," as the study was titled, typically went through a period of feeling anxious, scared, at loose ends, and as though they didn't belong. They variously described their states as "a vacuum," "in midair," "ungrounded," "neither here nor there," and "nowhere." This limbolike state results because we are still involved in the old roles though we know they are no longer viable. Yet we are unsure about what the future holds. Taking one or more last glances backward is necessary preparation for taking the leap forward.

Endings are tougher and take longer than we think. No matter how unhappy we may be in a job, most of us continue to revisit the possibility of making it work because the present role is necessarily tied to a possible self—an image, outdated though it may be, of whom we once wanted to become. June's academic identity, for example, kept reasserting itself throughout the entire transition period, even after she had handed in her resignation. "My department was family, a dysfunctional one," June says, "but one I was an intimate part of, one I joined at age seventeen when I went to college." For her, leaving academia meant not just giving up a long-term career objective but also an image of who she should become that important people in her life, including her mentor, harbored. The emotions she felt when she found the pile of draft articles that would have assured her professorial future show just how much giving up a possible self—even one that has become a burden or lost its appeal—marks a real loss.

Rarely does "becoming an ex" happen as a result of one sudden decision. Instead, it happens over a period of time, one that often begins before we are fully aware of what is happening. One study of divorce found that people who initiate the process of "uncoupling" are often not fully conscious that they are laying the groundwork for their exit.[5] But the signs of withdrawal are there early on, years before they become explicit. June's disengagement from the university and from her identity as a literature professor likewise began before even she realized she wanted a career change. Four years before her academic contract ended, she moved to New York City. Before her sabbatical, she had practically lived on campus; after it was over, she did not return to campus life.

Long before we start exploring alternatives, we also begin to disconnect socially and psychologically. A slow and gradual shift in reference groups—relevant points of comparison—starts to takes place. June, for example, began to identify with the values, norms, attitudes, and expectations of people working in the business world and began building relationships with people outside academia. The nuns in the "becoming an ex" study likewise began to cultivate relationships with laymen and -women, using these contacts to evaluate how they might adjust to life outside the convent. As their questioning of their religious commitment heightened, the nuns also intensified their contact with friends who had already left the order. A doctor on the brink of leaving medical practice, as reported in the same study, put it this way: "I was probably anticipating my move and beginning to build bridges so I wouldn't feel lost once I left my hectic involvement with patients."[6]

What typically ensues is mutual withdrawal: As the person who is leaving gets more and more involved in new activities and relationships, these begin to displace the old, and people in the old world respond in turn by loosening their involvement with the person who is leaving, asking and expecting less and less over time. June's colleagues attributed her diminished engagement to marriage and motherhood. She was no longer as available for lunches and extracurricular activities. Now that she had a "personal agenda," as her department head put it, she was obviously less committed to the scholarly life. Of course, this response only infuriated her, further motivating her to look for alternatives.

A cycle of mistrust developed between June and her colleagues in which, eventually, each interaction only reinforced her growing disdain for the academic world. Psychological distance, even rupture (what William Bridges calls "disidentification" and "disenchantment"),[7] is also part of the ending process. Often the rupture is personal; we experience a falling out with an important figure. When a relationship with a mentor deteriorates, or irreconcilable differences with our superiors arise, we experience more than mere disillusionment; our images of possible futures also change. June's academic identity was forged in relationship with her mentor; once her "personal agenda" interfered with his agenda for her, his support waned and so did the corresponding possible self.

In a memoir of her own career change, Harriet Rubin, a publishing executive, writes, "It takes, on average, three years from the time a person decides to leave the company until the day he or she walks out the door. Those are not good or productive years. For me those were three years in limbo."[8] Like her, most of us feel bad about postponing the break. But short-circuiting the unpleasant but necessarily unproductive middle period is counterproductive. "We need not feel defensive about this apparently unproductive time-out at turning points in our lives," writes Bridges, "for the neutral zone is meant to be a moratorium from the conventional activity of our everyday existence. In the apparently aimless activity of our time alone, we are doing important inner business."[9] Part of that inner business is the task of ending one thing; the other part of it—which takes longer—is creating substitutes.

Identities on Trial

One of the most striking things about June's in-between period was just how crammed with activity it was. Certainly she was doing the job of ending. But to get from the "in-between" to a "new beginning," we have to do much more than end well; we also have to create the possibilities that might replace what is being lost and find ways of evaluating the alternatives generated. As June's remarks about how to spend her Sunday show, when we are both fully engaged in the old role and trying to create a new life, we have a lot to do. During the between-identities period, we feel torn in many different directions. Although there are many moments of reflection, this is not a quiet period: A multitude of selves—old and new, desired and dreaded—are coming to the surface, noisily coexisting.

Like Gary McCarthy, the would-be scuba diver turned Virgin employee we saw in the last chapter, June played with a broad palette of possible selves: She looked at management consulting, knowing it was not for her; she considered whether or not to apply to other literature jobs; she took on a one-year volunteer project coaching high-school instructors to teach literature; she revisited the idea of moving into university administration; and she investigated a range of finance possibilities. As we will see below, oscillating among the different possibilities allows us time to come to new and different ways of integrating who we were then with who we are now and who we are becoming. When this self-exploration and self-testing ends prematurely—either because we are not able to tolerate the contradictions or because we are unable to assimilate new information about ourselves—we risk either letting go of the past too rapidly or holding on to it too rigidly.

How do we create and test possible selves? We bring them to life by doing new things, making new connections, and retelling our stories. These *reinvention practices* ground us in direct experience, preventing the change process from remaining too abstract. New competencies and points of view take shape as we act and, as those around us react, help us narrow the gap between the imagined possible selves that exist only in our minds and the "real" alternatives that can be known only in the doing.

Trial Activities

When June started playing with the stock market, she was not consciously testing a possible new career in finance. She was simply pursuing an interest that grew over time. But as her experiments in trading got bolder, her confidence grew and her self-image started to change. A literary person all her life, she had chosen words over numbers. As she devoured Web pages, watched the financial shows, and traded views with others on what to buy, she did not just nurture her skills; she also started to build a new, albeit tentative, identity, as someone who was "savvy about the stock market."

At first, she felt like an interloper. She did not belong in the career services center. Her interviewers would realize she did not have one iota of math training. She worried about coded signals, the unspoken rules of the game, from how to write her résumé to how to dress. She came from a field in which embroidered language was not just tolerated but rewarded and was surprised when early interviewers signaled their displeasure at her long-windedness. With practice, she learned: "The problem is not that I don't have a background in finance. It's that I haven't fully understood, in its entire nuance, the culture in which I want to live. With each interview, each e-mail, each phone call, I understand better what to do—and when to do nothing."

Along with learning about the kinds of jobs and companies that exist, getting a feel for herself in the concrete contexts and situations she was considering was critical. It was one thing for June to know she had done well in math as a teenager, for example, and quite another for her to work as part of a team in which others depended on her to come up with the right numbers. Each of these experiences provided her with different kinds of information. The former tells whether she has the aptitude; the latter tells whether she has the emotional constitution to enter a domain in which she will not be a natural from the start and whether she will enjoy working in such teams in the future. With her concrete actions, therefore, June continuously submitted the possible working identities to a test, learning more each time about the options she was creating. In making a career change, we become what we do.

Trial Relationships

Doing things—taking on new roles and projects—is one way to "try on" possible identities. Connecting with people is another. Making a major career change is not simply about picking up new technical skills and repackaging one's image and résumé. It is also about finding people we want to emulate and places where we want to belong. From beginning to end, June's story is punctuated by people she met who made a difference, from the day traders and stock-market speculators who inspired her at the start to the kindred spirits who gave her encouragement and advice along the way. Her desire to move into a career in finance and out of academia grew not as an abstract idea but as a tangible reality embodied in the people she did (and did *not*) want to be like.

Finding people with humanities backgrounds as well as finding women who seemed successful while still having time for their personal lives were, for June, critical tests of her options in the finance world. She made friends, for example, with her teaching assistant: "He considers that my working as a literature professor while taking business classes makes me as weird as he." At one investment bank, she was impressed with the physicist in fixed-income research who graduated from her university. At another bank, she met a managing director with an M.A. in philosophy and theology. She drew inspiration from the financial columnist, who like she, had a flair for writing. She especially enjoyed an economics course taught by a professor from Spain, a country where she had spent much time and in whose culture her academic discipline was rooted.

Each time June met someone from the new world she was seeking to enter, she ran them through the "Do I want to be like him?" and "Can I be like her?" tests. A "yes" led her to pursue the relationship—and the corresponding possible self—further. As we will see, our evolving working identities are also defined by the company we keep.

Trial Narratives

A working identity, however, is not merely what we do and with whom; it lies also in the unfolding story of our lives. Throughout a career transition, the narratives we craft to describe why we are changing (and what remains the same) also help us try on possibilities. June's attempts at explaining herself—why she wanted to make such a seemingly "crazy" career change, why a potential employer should take a chance on her, why she was attracted to a company she had never heard of a day before—were at first provisional, sometimes clumsy ways of redefining herself. But, each time she wrote a cover letter, went through an interview, or updated friends and family on her progress, she better defined what was exciting to her, and in each public declaration of her intent to change careers, she committed herself further.

Part of the difficulty she faced in telling her story to potential employers mirrored a very real dilemma: how to reconcile her ambition and her family responsibilities. Her desire to better provide for her children informed her desire for career change, yet she recognized that bringing up motherhood in her job interviews amounted to shooting herself in the foot. She came to understand that the most attractive places from a career standpoint would leave her little time for her family. So she experimented with different versions of her story, each time getting feedback on what her audience found plausible and what made her more or less compelling as a job candidate. Each retelling informed her evolving story.

Virtues of Variety

Once our possible selves are in play, what ensues can be likened to a fierce Darwinian competition taking place within ourselves.[10] Another reason the between-selves period is difficult is that, like June, we are juggling lots of different things—not necessarily with great coherence or consistency—often while still working full-time at demanding jobs. In evolutionary terms, we are "increasing variety." But, as our possible selves are fleshed out in deeper color and character, we begin to feel fragmented, not whole. We sometimes feel like an impostor in some, if not all, of the different lives we are leading. In a study of men who transitioned from conventional to artistic jobs, one participant expressed the stress of competing possibilities:

> *Then began a whole period of trying to compartmentalize my life and keep things going—to be a teacher, an artist, a lover, a husband, and father, and they were all kind of separate worlds. . . . I was faced with trying to bring it all together or simplify it by throwing some of them out. . . . My life exploded in a number of directions, a number of fragments, all of them contending for equal status.[11]*

As our possible-selves list grows beyond an intellectual exercise, we must next establish some means of selection. At first, the many possibilities are exhilarating. But most people simply cannot tolerate such a high level of fragmentation for an extended period of time. The time comes to reduce variety, to discard some possibilities, and to select, among them, a new favorite. How do we make the cut? We use information from two sources: our gut (our emotional reactions) and the people around us (their responses to our trials and efforts).

One barometer is an internal gauge: Can I see myself in this? Does this *feel* right? When June considered management consulting as a possible career, for example, everyone encouraged her, the possibilities were plentiful, and she was curious; but once she sat down to do a trial case, it became obvious that consulting was not for her. Working identity is not just who we are. It is also who we are not. Being able to discard possibilities means we are making progress.

The experiences of the transitional period also help us to sort out the confusing array of information and feelings about our past choices. June never once considered that she had made a mistake in choosing a literary career. It had been a true love, and she had done very well—*it was no mistake*. But to leave it behind her, she had to understand better why she wanted so much to abandon it. Her volunteer work with high-school teachers helped her separate her love of teaching, which remained unchanged, from her growing disenchantment with the university context and from the new circumstances in her life that had reoriented her professional priorities.

Having a range of tangible experiences to bank on helped her stay the course. When a job in her field became available at another university, June already knew intellectually that she did not want to continue as a literature professor. But she had not yet ruled it out unequivocally. The depth of emotional reaction against "the rational thing to do" (given that there was no alternative on the horizon) was sufficient data to finally cut off a branch of possibility that she had not yet put to rest. She realized then that she was willing to experience not knowing where she was going, choosing an uncertain outcome over an incremental improvement to her working life.

A second barometer is an external gauge, based on the feedback we get from those around us. In June's case, each interaction with the acquaintances, mentors, fellow students, potential employers, and professors who knew about her search for a new career made a difference. Others' reactions let her calibrate her own sub-sequent actions. People like the financial columnist James Cramer or the fellow students who read her résumé validated her efforts, suggested improvements, signaled acceptance and eventual mem-bership in her desired new profession, and, as such, shaped the person she was becoming.

This variation and selection process is not in the least an intel-lectual exercise or an introspective procedure. It is a physical ac-tivity in which we try on, in real time, any number of provisional identities. With feedback and validation, we might discard any one of these—or we might select one for a closer look.

Living the Contradictions

Well into her second semester of auditing M.B.A. courses, June followed her stockbroker's advice and applied for a position as a broker at Taylor Roberts. What at first had seemed so far from the world of Wall Street, so much less glamorous than private bank-ing, revealed a different set of advantages: independence, flexibil-ity, good training, good public schools for the girls, the prospect of buying a house with land around it, and a less stressful environ-ment in which to earn her stripes. The interviews took place in March. By the end of the month, she had accepted a job offer. A few days later, an offer from one of the top Wall Street banks came in. The recruiters were relentless in their efforts to persuade her to change her mind, but by this time, Plan B had become her favorite.

By the end of that summer, June had earned her SEC certifi-cation and had set up her office and business in a small New Eng-land town.

Taylor Roberts is turning out to be quite good for me, even if the culture shock was real at first. I have learned a lot, and as I go over material now, I am really understanding it better. I can make con-nections between different pieces of information that I could not make in the early going. My assigned mentor and regional leader have been very helpful, and my own stockbroker calls and checks in all the time! I am working all the time, every day, and am counting the good things already coming from it. Tonight I finish teaching my first investment class. It has been a lot of fun and has brought me to an obvious truth: I quite like teaching and I was sick to death of the university. I also gave another talk last week and am hoping to teach an investing course in Spanish.

After a year in the new job, June feels she made the right choice.

Once I became a wife and mother, my interests and values changed. My personal and intellectual life at the university had no importance compared with my wish to create an environment that would permit me a full dedication to my family—a real chance at making more money, giving my children good schools, being with them, and being with them out in the world in a way that would be consonant with my work life. This job gives me those things. Everywhere I go with the children—to their schools and their field trips—can and sometimes does lead to more business. All is joined together. There is no pull between the life of the mind and the life of the heart.

The between-identities phase of a career transition is about bringing possibilities to life, proving they are feasible and not just pipe dreams, and learning whether they are appealing in practice or only in theory. To discard outdated identities once and for all (that is, to do the work of ending), we need some good substitutes. Old possible selves are always more vivid than the new: They are attached to familiar routines, to people we trust, to well-rehearsed stories. The selves that have existed only in our minds as fantasies or that are grounded only in fleeting encounters with people who captured our imagination are much fuzzier, fragile, unformed. The middle period is the incubator in which provisional identities are brought, tentatively, into the world via the projects we start, the people we meet, and the meaning we lend to the events of that period.

What happens in this period sets the stage for the degree and success of one's reinvention. Whether it takes months or years, living the contradictions is one of the toughest tasks of transition. Indeed, living with uncertain identity can feel like "living inside a hurricane." But as we will see in the next chapter, premature closure is not the answer. People who can tolerate the painful discrepancies of the between-identities period, which reflect underlying ambivalence about letting go of the old or embracing the new, end up in a better position to make informed choices. With the benefit of time between selves, we are more likely to make the deep change necessary to discover more satisfying lives and work and to eventually restore a sense of continuity to our lives.

deep change

IN THE REINVENTING PROCESS, we make two kinds of changes: small adjustments in course and deep shifts in perspective. Often the first changes we make are superficial. We try moving into a new job, interacting with different people, picking up some new skills. Even when the need for a more profound change is apparent, its meaning can remain elusive. Small choices accumulate within a harder-to-change framework of ingrained habits, assumptions, and priorities. But after a while, the old frames start to collapse under the weight of new data. Sooner or later, the cumulative force of the small steps we have been taking requires a more profound change in the underlying framework of our lives.

That is not to say that small steps are inconsequential. In fact, they are often the only way to start tackling career problems that can otherwise overwhelm us. As we will see with Susan Fontaine's story, trying to make a big shift in one fell swoop can bring us back to square one all too quickly. Though it may feel at times like we are wasting time, taking two steps forward and one step back can allow a richer, more grounded redefinition of our working identity to emerge. If we interrupt the reinventing process prematurely, as Susan nearly did, we jeopardize our ability to fully internalize this new self-definition. Often it isn't until we are fairly far along in the reinventing process that we realize we must also reassess the foundations of our working identity. In Susan's case, she eventually discovered that there was much more than her job standing in the way of her achieving her stated goal—a better work-life balance—and that she needed to make a deeper change within herself to attain that balance.

Susan's Story

It was the day after Christmas and Susan Fontaine, a thirty-eight-year-old British executive with an M.B.A., had a sinking feeling. She had just left her job as partner and head of the strategy practice at a top management consultancy, partly because it did not allow her the family time she needed as a single mother of two. But it was, as she put it, "out of the frying pan, into the fire." She had accepted an offer for more of the same, this time as a senior executive at a top company in the United Kingdom.

> *I had been at Omega for about nine years, and through many changes. The original strategy partnership that I joined out of business school had been sold to a bigger company. Then we merged with a change-management consultancy. I had done quite well through it all, but when we started to prepare for another phase of restructuring, the same issues that had cropped up earlier reappeared; we seemed to have learned few lessons. Politically, many of my colleagues and I were feeling a bit exasperated with the company. Too often it seemed like we forgot the interests of our clients. I guess I had reached the end of my learning curve, too. I was thinking about leaving, but because I had been working so hard and I had two small children, I didn't really know what I could do, not to mention what I wanted next. I was clear,*

though, that I didn't want to just go on to another big consul-
tancy and do the same thing in a new company.

I found headhunters unhelpful, basically. I would ask, "Here
are my skills; what else might I do?" And they kept saying, "Why
don't you move to Andersen" or "Why don't you try Bain?" All
they could suggest was exactly the same thing. I kept saying, "I'm
quite clear I don't want to do that, and if I did want to do that, I
would not come to you. I can do that on my own." It was not a
valuable process.

The only thing I could come up with was some kind of corpo-
rate planning job, something close to what I was doing but, I
imagined, with less travel and fewer hours. I hadn't had any time
yet to look around or do research. I just had some fairly straight-
forward preferences about lifestyle. I wanted to work full-time but
without the globe-trotting that consulting required. I had been
clear with the headhunters about that, too, but they were still pro-
posing jobs that were clearly going to require me to travel around
the world recommending things that would be helpful to no one.

A former client heard that I was looking and approached me
with an offer. I was so flattered and had so little time to think
about it that I ended up going along with the interview process.
It was a terrific company, exciting. I had worked with them, so I
knew the director of strategy and I enjoyed the company. I guess
I thought it would be a good career move—I was pursued so as-
siduously, and he made it clear early on that he wanted me. I told
him I was moving out of consultancy because I didn't want the
relentless pace and traveling. I thought we had understood each
other. So I took the position, as head of strategic projects.

Almost immediately, I knew I had made a mistake. The day I
arrived, I found that my diary had been filled, and a lot of the as-
signments were abroad. Yes, I wanted a responsible job, but I did
have two small children whose lives had already been compromised.
I could see there was going to be no more latitude than there had
been in the previous job—probably less, because I didn't have the
reputation in the new company that I had had in the old.

I thought, "What have I done?" I had had the opportunity to leave all that. I had not explored my options thoroughly. I hadn't changed jobs in a long time. I didn't have the courage to actually take a break and allow myself some space. I just moved into the next thing and never allowed myself time to properly step back and consider what else I might do, whether this was what I wanted.

I stayed two weeks. Initially, I thought it would only be fair to stay on for a while. I had made a commitment. After a few days, I decided that it was either two weeks or two years, because I was beginning to work on proposals that were just ramping up. It was better to get out at the beginning.

Also, if I stayed, I wouldn't solve the problem. I was in the wrong place. It was unnerving because my CV, my experience, and, to some extent, my orientation were a perfect fit for this big job. I almost hesitate to say this, but some of it was certainly about work-life balance. In one sense, yes, it was sort of a "mommy's choice." But I think it was also about values. My integrity had been compromised at Omega, and here I had moved to yet another big, very political company, in which the internal wrangling did not always amount to the right thing to do. So it was partly a balance thing, which probably gave me the urgency to say, "No, this is wrong," but it was also a fundamental lack of comfort with how decisions get made in the corporate world.

Recently divorced, there was no second income to cushion the impact of Susan's decision.

Quitting felt like stepping out of an airplane 80,000 feet up without a parachute. I was in shock. Not that I regretted it, but I guess I doubted my judgment. I asked myself, "Why did I accept the job when it wasn't right?" I also wondered, "If this isn't right, what is right?" I didn't want to go back to the handful of people I had been talking to about jobs. I wanted some space. But I felt quite a bit of financial pressure, too. I knew I would have to work again pretty fast, but I also knew that the feeling of having to move instantly on to the next job, not spending very long deciding, had doomed me. I had the wits to see I needed some time out to have a think.

Over the holiday period, at the usual Christmas parties, Susan had seen many old clients who, intrigued by her move, promised to call for lunch. When they did phone in the new year, and Susan announced that she'd quit the job, many proposed freelance projects. That turned out to be the platform she needed. "I wasn't even thinking about doing freelance work. I was thinking about having some space. But actually picking up a couple of those jobs with a sense of 'Let's get back up on the horse again,' without expecting it to be a long-term solution, was a very good thing."

Susan's first freelance projects were in the same line of work she had been doing. She quickly discovered that she could get back up to the same income level, on an independent basis, without difficulty. No longer feeling that the wolf was at her door, she used her independence to do some things she had always wanted to do. She contacted one or two charities that she had previously supported to volunteer help in her areas of expertise, marketing and strategic planning. This led to her involvement, on a pro bono basis, with Sight Saver International. Susan helped the nonprofit with a big fund-raising campaign. It also turned out that they were hoping to diversify their trustee board with younger, more business-oriented representatives and a more balanced mix of men and women. Susan signed on.

I was freelancing, mostly for former clients, and doing charity work, which I didn't see as professional work. It was my lifeline during that period of ambiguity. After about two years, my "gift work" became my main line of work. The first step came after a few months, when I realized I would not look for another permanent job. I was doing well financially and enjoying the freelance lifestyle. I would not have chosen a freelance career— wouldn't have risked it—had I not gone through that two-week experience. But once I started doing it, I found it actually suited me very well.

After a couple of years, when it was clear that I was making a good living, that I was able to get quite interesting work, and that my network was serving me well, I began thinking, "Well, is this really *what I want to do?" I liked the independent lifestyle, but it was the same kind of work, with the same values. Through my pro bono charity work, I began to develop contacts for more paid charity consulting. That probably came about two years after I started freelancing.*

For now, I am working with the largest U.K. consulting firm that specializes in charities. The firm has helped me launch myself in the sector. It's probably a temporary passage to the next stage, which will certainly be in the charity area, because I enjoy that enormously. It could be as an independent contractor or as a full-time employee, on the consulting side or on the line side. All I hope is that I never again make the mistake of jumping before giving myself the chance to explore what I really want to do.

Small Wins for Big Change

Susan took a major misstep at the start of her journey by accepting a job that was old wine in new bottles. Like so many of us, she started her career transition without a clear idea of where she was going, and she was driven by an almost primal need to escape an untenable work situation. Between the uncertainties of the in-between period and the comfort of what should have been a "great job," she chose the latter. But the choice, a bold move to be sure, was immature because she made it without fully understanding the system of values and assumptions that led her there in the first place.

By the time she left her consulting firm, it was obvious to Susan that her priorities and preferences for the future were changing. What was not so obvious was the ambivalence she felt about deviating from what she called the "relentless logic of a post-M.B.A. CV." She was equally ambivalent about making a "mommy's choice." The inconsistencies between what Susan said she wanted and the choices she kept making created fault lines in her evolving life. Taking the wrong job led to the first "crack" in a tight system of interlocking assumptions and priorities that, consciously or not, had always informed her career decisions. But without having had time to explore options, to experiment, to assimilate discrepant experiences, the mistake simply made her doubt her judgment. She still could not see her own responsibility for the out-of-whack work-life balance, hence she was unable to fully make use of the new information about herself to take stock of past events or identify future steps. So, sensibly, she put decision making on hold and instead embarked on a long march toward an uncertain destination.[1]

Actions that reveal vividly and clearly who we *don't* want to be are important but insufficient. Unlike Gary, who kept looping back to his "conformist" list (or June, who revisited the idea of staying at the university in a different capacity throughout the transition process), Susan, thanks to her mistake, was able to discard her corporate possible self pretty quickly. From there, a hypothesis started to form: "Maybe a 'normal' job search can't get me to where I want to go," she said to herself. But to learn the next batch of relevant self-knowledge, Susan could not rely on historical self-reflection only, on sifting through her past. She had to move back into action mode. Her moratorium on using headhunters to seek a ready-made job made room for a more playful approach to her time and led her to stumble, accidentally, onto the nonprofit sector.

Not wanting to repeat her mistake, Susan changed her search rules; she abandoned the idea of making a big change, once and for all, in favor of taking a series of small steps just to see where they might lead. She created a portfolio of projects—some to pay the bills, some to explore new directions, and some, like the nonprofit work, simply to invest time in something she enjoyed doing. Originally, her nonprofit work was her "lifeline," a source of enjoyment and meaning in an otherwise difficult period. Gradually she found herself immersed in an industry in which she never expected to work for a living. And she found herself enjoying a style of work—freelancing—that she began only out of necessity.

Seemingly small steps, *changing one project at a time*, create momentum. Social scientists have argued that a strategy of "small wins"—making quick, opportunistic, tangible gambits only modestly related to a desired outcome—is in many instances the most effective way of tackling big problems.[2] Part of the reason small wins can produce much bigger results than a grand strategy is psychological: Defining a problem as "big and serious" can make us feel frustrated and helpless and therefore can elicit a less creative (or more habitual) response. We become paralyzed. We make the wrong move just to change. When we see change as requiring "big, bold strokes," we amplify our fear of it; we overcome this fear by putting one foot in front of the other, in a series of safer steps.

Small wins are also great ways to learn and to enlist supporters. Negotiating both a good fee and a limited travel schedule on her first consulting contract, for example, helped Susan discard barriers and discover resources that were invisible to her before. One small win in itself may not seem like much; a series of them increases the likelihood of serious change by setting in motion a dynamic that favors a next step and makes the next solvable problem more visible.

In Susan's case, the first problem to solve was staying afloat financially. Next came how to grow her network and how to work out more flexible arrangements. Each step revealed new information, which, in turn, changed the parameters of her search. She spent two years in the in-between period, oscillating between old and new ways of working and between private- and nonprofit-sector professional communities before coming back around to the question, "What do I really want to do?" When she again stepped back two years later to reflect on what she wanted, this time she had a store of relevant and immediate experience to inform a positive choice.

Dropping the Rocks

Like many who switch careers, Susan's transition brought her back to her starting point: working full-time for a top consultancy.

Yet her professional life—the way she does her work, the way she relates to coworkers and employers, and the way she balances her personal and professional life—has changed because of what she learned along the way. Making a career move is a chance to make fundamental changes in one's life. Many people, like Susan, have long-held dreams about their careers but for one reason or another—including financial, family, or social pressures—have put them off. In some cases, like Susan's, the issue is less the *substance* of the work than the *lack of flexibility* of the institutional structure in which the work gets done. In other cases, a person may have dreamed of becoming a writer, musician, or entrepreneur, but the practicalities of life were constraining. Still other people experience the deeper problem as an issue of authenticity, finding themselves caught in work situations that ask them to suppress too much of who they are in order to fit in. Whatever the cause, a time comes when long-ignored values, priorities, and passions reassert themselves—or the inconsistencies in our lives grow too blatant to ignore.

Elizabeth McKenna, who wrote about the life and career changes of women struggling to balance work and personal life, tells a parable about a woman swimming across a lake with a rock in her hand. As the woman neared the center of the lake, she started to sink from the weight of the stone. People watching from the shore urged her to drop the rock, but she kept swimming, sinking more and more. To the gathering crowd, the solution was obvious. Their "drop the rock" chorus grew louder and louder with her increasing difficulty staying afloat. But all their yelling did little good. As she sank, they heard her say, "I can't. It's mine."[3]

McKenna uses this story of a drowning woman to illustrate how stubbornly we can hold ourselves back. Susan, in fact, had many "rocks." One was her definition of a good job and, therefore, a good career move, what she called the "relentless logic of a post-M.B.A. CV." That rock was made heavier by her ambivalent feelings about sacrificing her ambition in order to be a better parent. Another rock was her fear of not having enough money, an understandable but untested fear. Although she knew what deep change she sought—better balance, greater meaning—when a job came up that allowed her to hold on to the rocks, she convinced herself that it was a good move.

Dropping our long-held assumptions, however, is not a simple matter of letting go once and for all. We are usually dealing with a mixed bag of preferences, priorities, and habits, some that we should hold on to and others we should jettison. When she first left her old job, Susan assumed that the problem was in the nature of consulting and not in her own attitudes and behavior. As she gained experience with new ways of working, she also learned new information about herself and eventually came to a more measured appraisal of the personal needs that triggered her desire for change in the first place.

Experience reveals barriers to change that we can rarely identify at the outset of a career transition, no matter how much self-reflection we do. What we see as feasible and appealing is always constrained by the limitations of our experience. Susan's story is not only about discovering a true passion for her work and a more balanced lifestyle. It is also about unlearning the assumptions that lead to the "next logical" and *absolutely wrong* move—in her case, untested assumptions about what kind of work produces a good income and what kind of job allows work-life balance. Dan McIvy's story below illustrates that as we explore possibilities, we start to recognize, question, and eventually dismantle some of the basic operating principles that are at the foundation of our working identities: what kinds of relationships we develop with the institutions in which we work and with our colleagues, and what kind of balance we strike between our private and professional lives.

Dan's Story

After a successful career as a turnaround specialist, Dan McIvy, a forty-seven-year-old computer scientist, left one of the top jobs at Beta, a leading computer manufacturer, with a new assignment: to turn his life around. As a young man, Dan knew his path to a better life would require hard work and an education. That path led him to push himself from one achievement to the next until the day he started to ask himself why he was so driven and what it was costing him. "It's sad to say," he later reflected, "but my only reaction to each success was that we could have done better."

As an enlisted man in the U.S. military, Dan attended night school and earned a B.A. in history. After completing an M.S. in computer science, he went into microprocessor design and earned a Ph.D. in engineering from Kyoto University. After the Ph.D., he started a joint venture with Matsushita to build Sun-compatible computers. The venture grew to $60 million in annual revenues but ultimately failed. Dan returned to the United States as vice president of hardware development at Data General. But during his time there, the company plummeted from its position as a market leader. From there Dan went to Beta, where he first managed its multibillion-dollar desktop business before moving on to turn around the troubled portable computer division.

As head of the portable group, Dan was credited with taking the business from under $1 billion to over $5 billion in annual revenues. Then it was split into two separate businesses and his responsibilities divided.

> *The personal computer business outgrew me. I wanted to quit then and there. But I got a psychological profile that helped me understand that I needed to stick it out and make it a success. The psychologist said I needed a big "success" in the business world. I had been successful as a chip designer, but the company I started was a failure. I went to Data General with big visions but the company didn't want change.*

He stuck it out at Beta but started thinking about a transition plan.

> *It was all part of a personal growth and transformation process. You do a lot of psychological self-assessment tests at Beta. Most are drivel. Even with the good ones, you ignore the input because*

you have been successful. I had feedback on my ruthlessness and arrogance. My reaction always was, "Okay, you go and do that job, then come back and tell me about it." Then one day I went to a "tree-hug" course. It was great. I had to write a personal mission statement. I wrote that I wanted to grow personally and to enjoy my children while priming a business at Beta. Then I realized I was using work as my escape vehicle from a dysfunctional marriage. I decided I wasn't going to miss out on my kids just because I had a bad marriage. I was driving my world at a frenetic pace, keeping things going so I wouldn't have to deal with this problem at the core of my life.

At Beta I made more money than I will ever need. But I rationalized the need to keep going. "I have to provide for my family," I said to myself. I still had a view of myself as the enlisted guy. I think I also feared the void I knew I'd feel once my life was no longer dictated by my company. At Beta, I was given a schedule every day that had meetings all day on it. If I did everything on the schedule, that was a good day. You don't think to ask, "What do I want to accomplish today?" Once I decided to leave, I had to figure out for myself how to fill that void.

Dan gave one year's notice, to give himself time to find a successor. As a lame duck, he faced an instant loss of prestige and exclusion from the inner circle. Episode after episode, and the depth of emotion each generated, drove home how much he relied on his title for a sense of self-worth. "Who am I, if not my job title?" was an open question.

One idea he began to explore during his last year at Beta was graduate study in organizational change, an area in which he could both apply and learn from his own experience. But everyone advised against doing a second doctorate, suggesting instead that he explore part-time teaching at one of the many business schools that used seasoned executives to expose students to the practice of management. He investigated programs on the Web, piquing the interest of a professor who wanted to form a virtual team of academics and business practitioners to teach leadership courses. Thanks to a simple cold call, he landed a part-time teach-ing and course development role at a prominent business school.

It seemed an ideal transitional solution. Dan had always wanted to teach. Since his priority was to spend more time with his children, he was also drawn to the flexibility of a part-time role. In the meantime, he had the time to coach his girls' soccer team and do all the other "dad" things he had previously missed out on. But even then he doubted his own motives.

I wrestled with who I am. I wondered if coming to a top-rated business school was more of the same, equating my value with the position. There's the "big me"—the person I want to be—and the "little me"—the petty self that needs crutches to go through the transition, the me that asks, "What would Mom say about me being a professor here?"

He struggled to understand his drive. "Why do I still feel a need to do more? Obsessive workaholism isn't healthy. I don't like being driven by an unknown force. I want to get to the root of it. Why do I always have to be doing instead of just being?" With the slower pace came a deeper awareness of how much his childhood affected how he had approached his career. "I realized that 40 percent of my peers grew up like me, in alcoholic families. We be-came overachievers, always trying to do more. We never feel we're good enough."

The more he probed what was driving him, the more Dan sought to understand his heritage as the child of an alcoholic.

I went into the Al-Anon program to get help resolving some of the issues that came from living with an alcoholic in my formative years. I'm amazed at how much I'm seeing and how it's been right in front of me the whole time. Either I wasn't ready before or it didn't speak to me in the right voice. The myth that I had control, that I could impose my will on the universe, was so deeply em-bedded that I didn't even know that there was a world of faith. Consequently, I never understood some of the basic tenets of life.

Of course, I'm only beginning, but it's really exciting. Once you head down the path of discovery, there is no going back. Who in their right mind would want to live unconsciously?

As he reflected on his life, Dan also experimented with how to help executives reach a higher self-awareness. "In class, I would move into a discussion of the emotional issues that businesspeople aren't supposed to talk openly about, using three specific examples from my experience: the loss I felt when the business was segmented, and my sense of failure despite objective success; the difficulty I faced in balancing my family and my career; and my experiences equating self-worth to position and title." As part of the thought process, Dan also decided to write about his transition. "I don't know if it will be of value to others, since it's so personal. I'm writing it for therapeutic reasons, and we'll decide what should come of the results."

About a year and a half after Dan left Beta, an attractive opportunity came his way, interrupting his moratorium on a search for a more permanent job. The offer was a trigger. It made him ask "the larger question of what do I want to do with the rest of my life." It was the chance to be the CEO of a company with exciting technology and great potential.

I was very excited because what this company needed was exactly what I do best, but it would take a large time commitment. I would still love to build a very successful company. But after thinking a bit, my decision was simple. I have the most important job that there is already, as a parent for my eleven-year-old twins. Their relationship with their mother has been volatile since our divorce, so I need to be the foundation for them. As I went through the decision-making process, I talked to the kids' counselor and to my old boss, who is now retired. Talking to him helped because I had deluded myself into thinking that if I built a strong team, I could have work-life balance and limit my work to forty or fifty hours a week. That really wouldn't have been possible. When I thought about what I could accept when I looked back on my life, I realized that I am totally at peace with missing the opportunity to build a great company and totally unwilling to miss my children growing up into strong, healthy people.

I was so pleased to have "passed the test." I firmly believe that as we go through life, we are taught certain lessons which we may or may not choose to learn. My need for external approval through achievement and accomplishment, along with the lack of balance in my life, were two lessons that I learned as I left Beta. Although I would have enjoyed the ego pump of being a CEO again—and I really believe that I could have done a great job—it wasn't worth the cost.

Exposing the Hidden Foundations

The difference between a job change and a career reinvention lies in a depth of personal transformation that is largely invisible to an outside observer.

When Dan first went to teach business part-time, he worried he had changed everything in order to end up the same—hooked on a big title that would signal his worth to the outside world. The time away from his high-powered executive job helped him to understand in a much more tangible way how much he had allowed his job and title to define his identity. He then shifted his priorities by organizing a part-time work schedule around his children, and he took a temporary assignment to tide him over. Seeing he was still drawn to high-prestige institutions and to projects that fueled his achievement overdrive brought him to the next question: "Why am I so driven?" He tried to approach this question in a number of different ways—by using his own experience as a case study in teaching executives, by writing about his career, and by exploring his family heritage at Al-Anon. The idea that he was looking for a much more profound change crystallized when a tempting job offer interrupted his self-imposed moratorium. As his story continues to unfold, he must figure out how to reconcile a challenging job in which he can make a meaningful contribution, with a family life in which he can fulfill his duty—and his dreams—as a parent.

Both Dan's story and Susan's illustrate that working identity involves revisiting the *basic assumptions* we use to evaluate possibilities. To illustrate what basic assumptions are, it is useful to think of our career choices as a pyramid with three levels (see figure 4-1).[4] At the top of the pyramid lies what is most visible, to us and to the outside world: what job we hold in what setting. Dan, for example, was an executive in a high-tech company. One level below are the values and motivating factors that hold constant from job to job and company to company. These are what MIT career specialist Edgar Schein calls our "career anchors," the competencies, preferences, and work-related values that we *would be unwilling to give up* if forced to make a choice.[5]

Dan's experience has led him to value himself professionally as someone who excels at turnarounds—at making troubled companies healthy. He could perform this role on a smaller or larger scale (for example, big company or small start-up), in an advisory or a hands-on role, and as a manager or an owner, but the constant is that managerial challenge is what excites him. Dan's turmoil over the offer of a "perfect job" that would have again robbed him of his family time, however, belies a conflict between his professional and personal values that is rooted at a deeper level. In his search, therefore, he has to plumb deeper: He must explore the final, bottom level of the pyramid to understand the basic assumptions—our mental maps about how the world works—that truly drive his behavior.

Even though our basic assumptions often remain hidden from our conscious awareness, they nevertheless determine how we manage our careers. Too often we fail to question them, even if they are obsolete or wrong. Precisely because they are taken for granted, basic assumptions are very hard to change. When they remain implicit, we only make incremental change. We only move from one situation into another that is superficially different. The organization or even the industry and sector may change and the coworkers

FIGURE 4 - 1

Levels of Career Decision Criteria

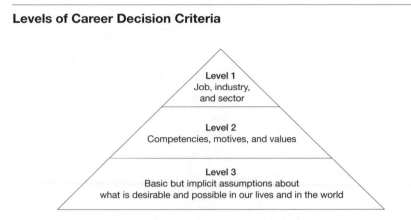

may be different, but in the end, we fall back into similar roles and relationships, reproducing the same work and life structure we had before. Why?[6] Because our working identity has remained the same.

In career transitions, the basic assumptions that typically prove most resistant to change concern our emotional relationships with institutions, our benchmarks for success, and our preconceived notions about viable work arrangements. To illustrate these, we will use the stories of many different people—some of whom we have met and some of whom we will meet in later chapters—who managed to attain a deep change.

Our Titles, Our Selves

Harris Roberts, a manager who had endured disappointment after disappointment in his quest for a broader role at his company, Pharmaco, didn't really come to understand what had held him back for so long until he witnessed reactions—his own and others'—to his decision to leave. His decision to take a job as the operating officer of a much smaller health-care company opened his eyes to the unhealthy attachment he held to his longtime employer and to how deeply he was looking for a different kind of connection.

When I worked at Pharmaco, I was Pharmaco. I felt like I em-
bodied the company, that I did everything the Pharmaco way. I
was their poster boy, literally: I was on their orientation videos,
talking about what Pharmaco meant to me. People used to say,
"You bleed Pharmaco blue," and I felt proud of that, because I'd
been there so long and the company meant so much to me. Now,
here at my new firm, I'm really dedicated to the vision and to
growing the company. But it's a completely different angle. I'm
dedicated to myself and my own personal goals as they relate to
what can I do for this company. Instead of "being the organiza-
tion," now I'm thinking, "What do I want this organization to
be? Let me test myself and see what I can do." It's more mature.

Psychologists who study adult development would agree that
it's more mature. Many people in transition, like Harris and Dan,
stumble onto the fact that they derive much of their sense of identity from their title and employer and that such overidentification
with any institution can lead to stunted growth in other arenas. Far
into our careers, we can remain the victims of other people's values
and expectations. Susan, for example, worried that peers would
think she was downshifting from an ambitious consulting career for
the mommy track. When she accepted the wrong job, she got lots of
validation: Everyone wanted her business card and asked her to have
lunch. Becoming our own person, breaking free from our "ought
selves"—the identity molded by important people in our lives—is
at the heart of the transition process.[7] So is ridding ourselves of an
unhealthy overidentification with the organizations that employ
us, a harder-to-recognize but equally problematic self-definition.

One of the reasons it is so hard to change careers—or why we
change, only to end up in the same boat—is that we can so fully internalize our institutional identities, relying on them to convey our
worth and accomplishments to the outside world. Even when we
can honestly admit that the external trappings of success—titles,
perks, and other markers of prestige—don't matter much, we can,
like Harris, hide from the need for change by telling ourselves how
much the company needs us. Like Dan, who postponed vacations

and overrode family obligations when the organization needed him, most working adults organize at least some portion of their working lives according to the principle that self-sacrifice is OK when it's for the good of the institution. Since basic assumptions tend to exist in interlocking clusters, what may often appear to be a work-life balance problem, or an inability to extricate ourselves from unrewarding or overly political working relationships, is in fact our inability to separate our commitment to an organization from *being* the organization.

Who Sets the Terms?

John Alexander left a senior position at a major investment bank to become a novelist. He later found himself, to his great surprise, doing financial advisory work part-time for a mix of old and new clients. This was not his intention, but when he left his old role, several clients asked him to stay on as an adviser. His first surprise was that they would be interested in hiring *him*, rather than the company brand name. Once that was settled, the next surprise was that they were willing to forgo the traditional rules that define relationships between professionals and their clients:

> *The first thing I said to them was, "You've got to understand one thing. I will do my best to be available to you, but forget the convention of the bank, that if you had a big enough whatever, we would drop everything—cancel vacations and so on. I'm not going to do that anymore. If I'm going away for a month to write a book, believe me, I am going away for a month to write a book. And by the way, dear chief executive, I know that if you've got a vacation, you take it. Even if you are working on a big merger, you work your way out of the office. Let me tell you, I'm having vacations too." What I found was that instead of saying, "Oh well, in that case don't bother," they all actually laughed and said, "We've always thought most of you investment bankers are lunatics." And it actually put me, more than before, on an equal footing with them.*

For John, leaving the bank, and therefore losing the brand and the title, allowed him to lose the basic premise of a client-adviser relationship: round-the-clock service. With that went all the other unexamined premises that had structured his working relationships. Even though his primary motive for leaving was a desire to write, John was also ready to leave a career empty of meaning and marked by tiresome political struggles among the partners at the bank. And he couldn't abide the commercial logic that had limited his relationships with clients. Once he realized how much he could enjoy advisory relationships, redefined by his new working rules, he began to experiment with other ways to change the terms, especially his mode of working with peers to deliver financial advice.

In the end, John created a virtual organization that defies the typical investment bank team loaded with junior analysts whose job it is to "leverage" the time and ideas of the senior partner. "It has evolved so now there are eight of us, all very part-time. I set it up so there were no offices and no salaries, apart from the secretarial support. We're all equals. We refuse to give any reports in writing or do any PowerPoint presentations." Has John made a career change? If one looks to his novel writing, the answer is obviously yes. If one looks at his financial advisory work, what lies at the top and middle of the pyramid looks similar. But at the foundation John has reconfigured everything.

"Work-life balance" has become a preoccupation precisely because it is so hard to achieve. Correcting the encroachment of work on personal life is a pressing concern for most professionals seeking change, whether or not they are conscious of it at the start. But Dan McIvy and Susan Fontaine found that correcting the imbalance is not such a simple matter because it is part of a larger system of basic assumptions that reinforce each other. John's autonomy—and therefore time for all the other things he wanted apart from advisory work—increased not just by virtue of his setting his own schedule; rather, it came with his freedom from other people's expectations for what kinds of jobs he should hold and how he should do those jobs.

Practice Makes Perfect

Most of us know what we are trying to escape: the lockstep of a narrowly defined career, inauthentic or unstimulating work, numbing corporate politics, a lack of time for life outside work. But finding an alternative that truly fits, like finding our mission in life, is not a problem that can be solved overnight. It takes time. Whatever the first step, the process gradually changes the nature of what we know and what we seek to learn. Learning happens in cycles. Early cycles focus on the most immediate (or surface) problems. Later cycles provoke the bigger questions: How do I put it all together? What other facets of my life do I need to adjust?

Even when we start a career transition with these deeper questions in mind, it can take time to discover what we truly want to change. Trying to tackle the big changes at the beginning can be counterproductive. Our customary mind-set about who we are and what others expect undermines us in myriad subtle ways. Just as starting the change process by trying to identify one's true self can cause paralysis rather than progress, starting by trying to change basic assumptions inevitably leads to an exercise in abstraction and, all too often, avoidance of real change. We are simply not equipped to make those deeper changes until we come to understand what they really mean, not as concepts but as realities that define our daily lives.

Transformation, then, happens less by grand design or careful strategy than by the small wins that result from ongoing practices that enhance our capacity to change. As part 2 of this book makes clear, getting from an often clumsy or superficial first effort to the deeper changes we seek is a matter of working and reworking identity as an ongoing practice. Practice makes perfect, eventually allowing us to reaffirm certain fundamental truths about ourselves and to anchor those with new premises that will guide us in the next phase of our professional life.

part 2

identity in practice

crafting experiments

B Y FAR the biggest mistake people make when trying to change careers is to delay taking the first step until they have settled on a destination. This error is so undermining because, as we have seen, we learn about ourselves by doing, by testing concrete possibilities. And few of us change careers from one day to the next. We don't, as a rule, leap into the unknown. Instead, most of us build a new working identity by developing the girders and spans as "side projects"—extracurricular ventures that allow us to test possible selves without compromising our current jobs.

Crafting experiments refers to the practice of implementing the small probes and projects that allow us to try out new professional roles on a limited but tangible scale without committing to a particular direction. This chapter will show many ways to set up experiments that work. As Ben Forrester's story illustrates, this experimental method is not just a means of exploring known possibilities; it is also a way of creating unforeseen ones. Moreover, experimenting is not a one-shot deal: It is a method of inquiry, one we can use to confirm or disconfirm our hunches about what options are feasible or appealing. Experiments allow us to flirt with our possible selves.

Ben's Story

There was no grand plan, just a deepening of involvement over time. About three years ago, when I looked at how I was spending my time, I could see that my priorities were shifting. I was spending less and less time on the projects that were going to get me promoted as a professor. I was spending more and more time on my outside activities, and especially on nonprofit consulting projects. Eventually, I was offered the job of managing partner of Connector, a nonprofit start-up. If I said no to this opportunity, I was not sure I would ever say yes to anything, and that really made me stop and think. It was a tailor-made situation.

Since his days as a graduate student, Ben knew the academic world was a less-than-perfect fit for him. He loved the intellectual stimulation of his field, organizational design. Institutions and their problems fascinated him. But he found research lonely and writing laborious. He enjoyed teaching, but he wished it took less out of him. He often found himself stressed and resenting the time and energy his career consumed.

A great advantage of being a professor at a prestigious business school, friends and colleagues kept reminding him, was that it provided a great "platform." He had the freedom to work on a variety of projects, and contacts and resources were abundantly available. So instead of exploring alternatives to working as a professor in a university—after all, he had invested six years in getting a Ph.D.—he built a portfolio of diverse outside activities including writing, teaching, consulting, and board work. Yet he knew, come promotion time, the academic up-or-out system was relentless in rewarding research exclusively.

Ben especially enjoyed the consulting work. Manworks, one of the companies he had been researching for a project on interim executive work, engaged him for strategical and operational help: "They let me play at the nitty-gritty. I always thought I'd enjoy a hands-on leadership role, and this helped me test that intuition."

Over the years, Ben had been involved on an informal basis with several nonprofits, providing advice and occasionally writing about them. Around this time, he joined the board of ReadNow, a nonprofit focused on the literacy of young children. Eventually, he became chairman of the board. In his nonprofit work, he found a hungry audience for his expertise—designing effective organizational structures and facilitating decisions about how to change. For his part, the urgent pace was a refreshing change from the plodding schedule of scientific research.

Simultaneously, a small side project Ben had started on nonprofit consulting bloomed into a full-scale research project when the university received a large grant to study nonprofits. All the pieces seemed to fall into place. "I used my research on designing multiunit companies to develop ideas about how nonprofits can achieve economies of scale. My first project was to study how one of the nonprofits I was involved with developed its growth strategy." The potential for impact was exciting and much more satisfying than a thoroughly researched article that only a handful of academics would ever read.

As he began his involvement with Connector, Ben also started to participate more and more in his school's nonprofit initiative. He was in a unique position to straddle the academic and nonprofit worlds. "I was leveraging both my academic knowledge base and my personal contacts. I've always had a quirky network, with no real core. In organizational research, I don't know many people, but I have been fortunate enough to know a few of the *right* people. The same goes for foundations. I had some high-level nonprofit contacts from my board activities and a few strong connections in that world. It's an eclectic network."

An old boss from Ben's previous job as a consultant after college, Tim Turner, asked him to work on a pro bono project researching an unmet need in the nonprofit market. As managing director of a top-tier strategy-consulting firm, Tim had noticed the skyrocketing demand in the nonprofit sector for specialized professional services such as consulting and financial advising. But the proportion of clients in the nonprofit arena was growing fastest.

Over the course of two years, Ben and Tim conducted in-depth interviews with leaders of nonprofits and foundations that revealed an insufficient supply of data-driven, analytical strategy consulting available to this sector at prices it could afford. Working closely together, Ben and Tim began to explore ways of meeting that need. A close mentoring relationship developed. "Working with him exposed me to a whole new set of skills—making compelling pitches, building a group, leading a small but complex organization. Tim is incredibly skilled at giving feedback and advice about things like dealing with the board. He said, 'My job is to help you.' "

Ben enjoyed his side projects more than his "day job," but he wasn't sure what to make of that. People close to him had opinions.

> *My wife always thought I was mismatched with my job. She was the impartial voice saying, "You should leave. You have more fun doing the outside things. Make that your job." She could see that I was not happy. The outside work engaged me in a way academia never did. And I knew I wasn't living up to my potential.*

With important deadlines looming for academic promotion, Ben had to dwell on the immediate future. He published a book on organizational design, based on his doctoral research; this won him promotion to associate professor. Souring this good news, he was told he had to focus. There were risks to his side projects, his superiors cautioned; if he wanted to make the next promotion, he had to invest in traditional research. And his colleagues had plenty of things for him to do—courses to teach, executive sessions to lead. Precious few of these assignments were in the nonprofit sector, a "hot" but still marginal domain for a traditional business school focused on private industry.

As Ben tried to think ahead to the next few years, he realized he had little energy or appetite for the next round.

> *I had gone through the associate professor promotion to prove that I could do the research. But, three more years of making sacrifices in what I wanted to do for the sake of tenure (the next*

promotion hurdle) seemed too long. I kept thinking about what else I wanted to do. And I was tired of feeling guilty about spending so many days out of the office. Many people said, "Just stay there and focus on nonprofits." But that ignored all the other stuff I had to do like teach introductory courses, participate on university committees, and advise M.B.A. and doctoral students. It was a question of what was peripheral to my real interests and what was core.

About the time of his promotion, one of Ben's biggest clients, Manworks, began to search for a COO. Ben considered pursuing it. But though the timing was good, the opportunity was not quite right. "Manworks had an inexperienced management team. That was going to limit what I could learn from them. Since I did not have a track record in managing, the absence of role models felt like a real drawback." Deciding not to pursue this, though, made Ben think long and hard about what kind of offer he would say yes to.

Meanwhile, the ideas he had been designing with Tim Turner were taking shape. They decided to create a separate organization to build the nonprofit consulting practice. Ben was deeply involved in developing the business plan. When the fledgling Connector was granted nonprofit status, Ben became a cofounder and managing partner of the start-up. This time someone was holding out a hand as Ben decided to step over to the other side: "Tim was willing to make a bet on me. He gave me the confidence that I would learn a lot from this opportunity. His presence made it easier to take the leap."

The Experimental Method

To craft an experiment is to act in order to see where the action leads. It is to ask the most basic question: "What if?" Experiments come in many forms: Some are unintentional, others are conducted by design, some are exploratory, others, confirmatory. Scientists use the term *natural experiment* to refer to situations that occur naturally, without experimental manipulation, yet allow a clean, comparative test. The fact that life events separate some but not all twins, for example, creates a natural experiment that can be used to sort out the effects of nature and nurture. But, in most cases, the only way to learn what we want to know is to design a test ourselves.

Exploration means taking action only to see what happens, without trying to make a prediction or test a hunch. An *exploratory experiment* is a probing, playful activity by which we get a feel for things.[1] Exploratory experiments succeed when we are able to formulate more specific questions, or when they lead us to a hypothesis or educated guess. Then comes a more rigorous test, a *confirmatory experiment*, in which the objective is to learn whether the hypothesis is supported or refuted by the evidence.

Let's take a closer look at Ben's experimental method. At the start, in that familiar "I'm not looking to change but something's missing" period, Ben pursued different interests and worked on various projects. He was not asking, "What if I were to do this for a living?" Not yet. But his experience revealed some patterns, confirming, for example, that he enjoyed having a hands-on role in an organization.

His natural experiments were simple "we talk with our feet" tests of his true inclinations. How Ben allocated his work time was much more telling *in deed* than anything he might have been able or willing to articulate *in words*. It was clear to him that he was spending more time outside the business school than inside. He was spending more time on nonprofit work than on academic research or consulting to for-profit organizations. And within the nonprofit realm, he was spending most of his time on the project with Tim. The aphorism "I know who I am when I see what I do" (a twist on Alice in Wonderland's famous words to the Red Queen[2]) proved true for Ben.

Natural experiments get the ball rolling. They give us a peek at possible directions. But they only take us so far. After a certain point, a hypothesis starts to materialize, and another kind of test is required. Exploratory experiments are designed to answer fairly open-ended questions: Would I enjoy doing *X*? Could I be good at doing *Y*? Would I be able to make a living doing *Z*? Once a possible self begins to take form, we need to take more active steps to test the possibility more rigorously. Otherwise, we stay in the realm of daydreams.

As his hunches about enjoying hands-on and nonprofit work strengthened, Ben sought more opportunities to do those things within the scope of his job as a professor. In fact, he began to see the advantages of pursuing his new interests from inside, rather than outside, the university. Realizing that his job was indeed a great platform, he explored a variety of business school roles and possibilities: He worked more closely with a new group created to study social enterprise, taught in a course for nonprofits, wrote a case study about new models for nonprofits, and attended conferences. As a result, his contacts in this new realm grew, and he saw, with increasing clarity, how well his expertise in organizational design applied to change leadership in the nonprofit realm. He created a new niche for himself. Now he had to figure out how to best exploit that niche and whether to do it as an impartial observer, as an academic, or as a player.

Compare and Contrast

In the exploratory phase of any investigation, looking into not one but a broad range of options is essential. Variety allows comparison and, therefore, discrimination: "This resonates and that doesn't"; "I like *X* better than *Y*"; "Even in the best of possible worlds, I really don't want to do *Z*." Thanks to the comparative method, Ben was able to refine his hypotheses about what was more and less appealing to him. For example, he realized that he preferred the short time frames and immediate feedback of his consulting work to the long horizons of a research career. He also learned something new: Impact really mattered to him. Neither academic work nor for-profit consulting made a direct difference in the world in the same way his nonprofit work did.

Since Ben had several experiments going (a good design principle, as we will see), he was able to continue comparing and contrasting experiences as he moved from exploration to confirmation. The comparative method allowed him to rigorously test alternative hypotheses about what he wanted. One test was the road-not-taken test. Ben had always kept the possibility of moving into a corporate managerial position (a common turn for business faculty who want a more hands-on role) on the back burner. When the Manworks position opened up, he was forced to respond to a possibility he himself had created. At that point, it became clear to him that he did not want it.

Ben's reaction to the Manworks opportunity helped him narrow his quest, and it also led him to reframe the questions guiding his search. Until then, his focus had been on the substance of the work: Which tasks do I enjoy most, and which do I enjoy least? What kind of work am I best at? What kind of work stresses me out? The road-not-taken test gave him insight into a set of drivers he had only been vaguely aware of. Since Manworks was not particularly well run, (that was why they needed him), he would be coming in as the expert, coaching them and exploiting a knowledge and experience base he already had rather than stretching himself. At Connector, it was the other way around. He was the protégé, at least at the start, and this assignment would allow him to grow. The mentoring he was getting from Tim made all the difference. In not pursuing Manworks, Ben realized he was not looking for a different job but rather looking for role models—people he admired, whom he wanted to learn from and work with.

The ability to compare and contrast also came in handy when Ben had to choose between doing the nonprofit work from his position as a business school professor and doing it as the new director of Connector. This was tough because, at least in theory, the substance was the same (namely, working with nonprofits). As is typical, some of his friends told him he was nuts to consider quitting such a good job. His coworkers told him they needed him, that in a couple of years he would get tenure; then, they argued, he could do anything he wanted. It made sense—except for two things. One was the toll it was taking on him, which his wife could see better than he. And, the other, as she pointed out to him, was that the substance of the work was *not* at all the same: Continuing as professor, even after tenure, would mean having to divide his time among many activities, most of which were peripheral to what had become his core interests.

So when an offer to run Connector materialized, Ben took it. Technically, it was yet another confirmatory experiment, since university rules allowed a two-year leave of absence, after which he could have his old job back. But the hypothesis was confirmed, and he resigned from the business school at the end of the two-year period.

Narrowing the Search

Early explorations like Ben's are smaller, faster, lower-cost investments than full-fledged career changes, cheap ways to gain insight into vaguely defined possibilities. They are projects, part-time ventures, and limited partnerships set up as low-risk ways to diversify a portfolio rather than "big bang" investments. With each experiment, priorities become clearer; we progress from open-ended questions to more serious tests. Crafting experiments allows us to move, even if gradually, from exploration to confirmation, the only way to avoid becoming stuck, like many would-be career changers, in the daydreaming stage.

One thirty-four-year-old New York business consultant, for example, never imagined he would remain a consultant for ten years. He always wanted to write history books, and his dream was to become a professor. This was his version of Gary McCarthy's scuba operation. But unlike Gary, he never put that possible self to the test. He failed to act on his dream, never discarding it or exploring it further. Every time a job opportunity came his way (since he was not actively seeking change, the options were close to his current line of work), it compared unfavorably with his cherished image of himself as a historian. To really *know,* to generate usable information vis-à-vis his dream career, he would have had to test his fantasy. He would have had to engage in activities and relationships that would uncover whether he liked doing history work, whether he was good at it, and, eventually, whether he could defy conventional wisdom and earn a decent living as a historian.

Exploration is about formulating hypotheses or best guesses; confirmation is about rigorously testing preliminary conclusions. Confirmation turns best guesses into sure bets. As in scientific discovery, the less we know about a phenomenon, the more open-ended our questions. As relevant knowledge builds up, we become more precise about what we seek to learn, and we start to anticipate (more and more accurately) what we will find. Because hypothesis-testing experiments (for example, taking a new job on a provisional basis) are usually more costly than exploratory experiments (for example, working on a side project without leaving one's job), we prefer to defer the former until we have solid data suggesting that we are going in the right direction.

Variety for its own sake is not enough. In fact, a prolonged exploratory phase can be a defense mechanism against changing, and it can signal to others that we are not serious about making change. A true experimental method almost always leads to formulating new goals and new means to achieve them. As we learn from experience, we have to be willing to close avenues of exploration, to accept that what we thought we knew was wrong and that what we were hoping to find no longer suits us.

Opening Gambits

What experiments can a person in transition devise to help guide future steps? How do we extract the right lessons? The practice of crafting experiments involves a two-part method: choosing one or two new activities to get started and making sure we have sound ways of evaluating the results. As we explore with more examples below, many different kinds of activities can yield useful and actionable information. But, to learn from our experiments, we must discipline both our reason and emotions, either of which can lead us to the wrong conclusions even in the face of compelling evidence.

Side Projects

Like Ben, many people start a new career, unintentionally, by developing new areas of expertise on the side while still working full-time in their current jobs. Like he, we experience a deepening commitment to the new area over time and find ourselves devoting more and more time to that realm. Only later do we have to decide whether to abandon the old path in order to follow the new.

Carol Brookline, a thirty-eight-year-old consultant in the United Kingdom, worked for years as a client adviser to an industrial food products concern before founding her own Web-based business. Typical of the entrepreneur who develops a business idea (often one linked to a day job) during spare time, Carol stayed on in the old job until she had enough evidence that the time was right to found her own company. Like Ben, Carol relied on several experiments to guide her, one step at a time. Following the small-wins approach, in which the strategy is to go for modest but quick outcomes, she tested her theories about both her preferences and business opportunities in steps. In so doing, she uncovered resources and barriers that were invisible to her before she started experimenting.[3]

Consulting to her client, Carol realized the potential of taking orders online. She also gained more exposure to a line-management role by working closely with the CEO and his senior executives. "This gave me the confidence that I could actually run something, that I could manage a senior team," she said. Another side project, a biotech start-up she launched with her brother-in-law, taught her how to negotiate with venture capitalists.

None of those were intended as moves toward a new career. But when she saw the most satisfying client relationship of her consulting career come to an end and realized that she would not be happy returning to a job selling new business and implementing short-term engagements, the side projects gave her a base. Remembering that she had vowed to herself that she would not "turn forty still a consultant," she moved into an exploratory phase in which she investigated three options. She did a feasibility study for the food business and explored two ideas in human resources and marketing. (These ideas came from projects she had worked on as a consultant.) As the research kicked into high gear, she gave six months' notice at the consulting firm, which allowed her to explore her options more fully and at her own, rather than her employer's, expense. Eventually, the first project beat out the other two as the preferred option.

Many professionals work on pet projects or outside professional activities that, over time, take on a life of their own. Among lawyers, investment bankers, and consultants who, like Ben and Carol, have moved into different sectors, intriguing possibilities often materialize from new clients, pro bono projects, and board memberships. By the time the actual break occurs, the "new" is well defined and the decision is informed by the fact that the new career is already launched.

Temporary Assignments

Not every job, however, allows the kind of flexibility needed to plunge into one or more side projects. For many of us, an exploration phase simply consists of networking, applying for jobs, looking at postings, or talking to headhunters. As we narrow the search, we might use temporary assignments, outside contracts, advisory work, and moonlighting to get experience or build skills in a new industry. For Jim Byers, taking a short-term post was part of an explicit job search strategy. After more than fifteen years of practicing anesthesiology, the forty-two-year-old Byers had had enough of life in Kentucky and the high-stress schedule that went along with hospital surgery.

I wanted something less burdensome. I was tired of working from seven in the morning to eleven at night, being on call, and worrying about getting woken up in the middle of the night and having to work the next day. So I started looking at anesthesia opportunities in Wyoming and Alaska, in small towns or rural areas. I took some time off to interview and work part-time in other places as a way of exploring possibilities. I worked up in Fairbanks, Alaska, for a few weeks and really fell in love with the area. If I was going to stay in anesthesia, which is what a reasonable person would have done, that was the job I was looking for. Then my wife became pregnant for the first time at age forty-two and didn't want to go to Alaska anymore. So I thought, "What do I want to do if I can't go to Alaska?"

That's when I started to think about a career in business. One of my friends, who had a law background, had been in Silicon Valley for seven years. He was actually making a transition himself. I called him up and said, "What do you think is the likelihood of someone with my background making a move to the health-care business?" He said, "What a coincidence—I've just taken a job at a Stanford start-up that provides knowledge systems to doctors. Why don't you come over, to see if we're a good match?" We agreed that I would come out on a volunteer basis. One or two weeks later, I went out for a month. I looked at it as a one-month trial. Then after a couple of weeks, when it looked like I could contribute to the business, I decided on a six-month trial. Eventually, he made me an offer and I accepted.

As Jim's experience illustrates, the experimental method does not necessarily entail an orderly sequence of steps in which one side project leads logically to a next. Instead, small probes are often fragmentary and spontaneous, driven by unexpected opportunities and dynamic situations. Jim's wife got pregnant and Alaska was out. What next? A different kind of experiment. Like Ben and Carol, Jim went for variety in designing his experiments. But the trend is clear: Small wins may be scattered, but what counts is that they move in the same general direction—away from the stifling situation we are trying to escape.[4]

Back to School

Taking courses or picking up training and credentials in a new area is still another way of experimenting. A leave of absence, sabbatical, or extended vacation can allow us experiences that improve our capacity to move in new directions.[5] Often an executive education program or its equivalent is enough to reorient a career; in other cases, evening or weekend classes taken over a longer period help us to orient a search and develop options.

Leif Hagstrom needed a time-out from his longtime career with a Norwegian financial services firm he had helped found.

> *I wanted a break. I thought of it as hitting the refresh button on Explorer. I was burned out, unenthusiastic. I wanted to go to the States. I checked out some executive development programs, like the Sloan Fellows at MIT and the Kennedy School Midcareer Program at Harvard. I realized, though, that taking a whole year off would mean leaving the firm. That was the cliff—I had a good job, a comfortable lifestyle, a good income. My partner was especially anxious about my going away. After much perseverance, I finally got him to agree to the ten-week executive program at Harvard.*
>
> *Being in the program was like living in a bubble. You have no worries, no stresses. It made me see that I didn't want to go back to my life in Norway. I realized life could be something else—less worrying, more enthusiasm. In my small group, only one person, a Japanese man, intended to go back to the same job. One guy said, "I know my bank will merge over the next year. They will kick me out if they can't use me. The loyalty is not there anymore." I myself had sacked some of our partners. Our professors told us, "All of you will have to change your business models in this changing world."*

Reason and consistency—what Susan Fontaine, the M.B.A. who jumped from one corporate job to another, called the "relentless logic of a post-M.B.A. CV"—keep people from thinking outside the box. One of the biggest advantages of going back to school, or taking any form of sabbatical, is that it makes room for play, allowing people "to experiment with doing things for which they have no good reason, to be playful with their conception of themselves."[6] Because the suspension of the rules is temporary (and legitimate—easy to explain to the people around us), a sabbatical demarcates a protected time and space in which we can safely toy with possibilities, knowing that we will have to come back to reality again.

Leif took courses that opened up new worlds. He learned about the Internet and about how to shake up a stodgy company. He found soul mates in other program participants and forged lasting relationships with some of the faculty. The separation from his partner gave him the opportunity to reflect on what *he* really wanted to change. With time and distance, Leif realized that he felt taken for granted by his partner. Before the program, he had simply wanted to "refresh"; the time away convinced him that the problem was not the work itself but a work ethic that left no room for fun and a junior role in his relationship with his partner that he had outgrown. A new, more confident, and more entrepreneurial working identity began to blossom.

What Leif ended up doing—joining a travel-business start-up in New York as chief financial officer—had little to do with his reasons for attending the program. But by virtue of his time away, he stumbled across (and prepared himself to seize) an opportunity he would not have imagined.

I came back after the program, pumped up to create change in my firm. I had been back one week when we entered a high-profile legal dispute with one of our biggest clients. The litigation swamped the whole summer and ruined my vacation with my family. It sucked out all the enthusiasm I had had coming back. On my way back to Norway from the States, the business partner of one of my old school friends, Peter, was on my plane. Carl and Peter had recently founded a U.S.-based travel company. While I was in the program, I had done a little consulting work for them, since the executive program had given me a direct pipeline to the latest business models. When I got bogged down in the same old thing again, I told Carl I was fed up. He said, "We need a CFO. Why don't you join us?" And then I just jumped. It was not a calculated move. I always thought that one day something was going to drift by and I'd grab it. I knew this was it.

Gutsy Thinking

Once we have tried our hand at some experiments, how do we evaluate their results? How do we decide which to pursue further and which to drop? All experiments, even the most preliminary, come at a cost. Ben, the professor turned nonprofit director, was aware from the start that his side projects would not provide the kind of résumé that would be rewarded by promotion at a "publish or perish" business school. Carol, who founded a food products company, had to sacrifice her full-time consulting job in order to research her three options. For Leif, the banker who went into the travel business, going to an executive program heightened his growing intolerance of his old job. When we craft experiments, we increase the likelihood that things will never be the same again. For this reason, we also need methods to evaluate what we are learning while minimizing the costs we incur in the process.

We all fear the blind spots that lead to bad choices. Our biases can lead us astray at many different points along the way, from how we frame identity questions to what we conclude from our experiments. Counterbalancing our natural biases requires a partnership of emotion and intellect—working with our subjective and emotional responses (our gut) as part of the analysis, yet submitting those responses to thoughtful challenge and criticism.[7]

Natural subjectivity can lead to what researchers call the "negotiating with yourself and losing" phenomenon.[8] This is the all-too-familiar experience of having two versions of ourselves, one "emotional" and one "rational"; one that knows what we "want," the other that knows what we "should" do. Like Susan Fontaine, who leapt too soon to the wrong next job, all too often our rational, "ought selves" take over, telling us to consider only a hard-nosed look at "the numbers," to ignore the rumblings of our guts. "Don't be emotional," they tell us. And in the name of rationality, we make the wrong choice. The lesson is not to throw reason to the wind. It is to trust emotional information, even when we can't articulate what our gut is telling us.

In *Descartes' Error,* Antonio Damasio showed just how rational it is to treat our emotional reactions as information.[9] Far from interfering with rationality, he demonstrated that emotion and feeling are critical to enlightened decision making. In one ingenious experiment, Damasio compared the gambling results of two groups: individuals with prefrontal-lobe brain damage, which keeps reason intact but blocks emotional reaction, and individuals without prefrontal-lobe brain damage. "Normal" people begin to make good choices before they realize, intellectually, what strategy works best; by contrast, prefrontal patients continue to make bad choices even after they recognize a winning strategy. We like to think that good decisions in complex situations—like tough gambling moves and vexing career choices—are founded on a solid rational process (get the facts, define the options, make an action plan). Damasio's studies show that emotional biases, the compass of the gut, guide behavior long before conscious knowledge sets in.

Larry Pearson, a thirty-five-year-old investment banker in New York who moved into international development, could have easily fallen into the "negotiating with yourself and losing" dynamic. As he started to investigate the nonprofit sector, which he knew virtually nothing about, he was downsized out of his job. What started as a welcome "kick in the butt" (he had already decided he wanted to move into the nonprofit sector) turned into a long and lonely search period. In his case, disciplining both rational and emotional reactions was critical.

It was a difficult process because I wasn't sure that I should stop interviewing with the banks. I had two commercial banking offers right away. I wasn't far enough along in the process to have received job offers from the nonprofits. So it was hard to turn the first offers down. They were great jobs. You're thinking to yourself, "How long is this going to take? Is it really going to lead to a major change?" But I made a commitment to try to enter this arena. It had only been two months, and I knew it would take longer to make a complete change. My friends thought I was bonkers.

With the nonprofits, the first hour of any interview was, "Why the heck would somebody with your background and your pay scale be doing this?" It took an hour's worth of credibility building; they weren't wondering, "What is your background, and what can you offer?" but "Are you insane?" Also frustrating was that I was often talking to people who came out of social services backgrounds. They didn't get the points I was making about finance. Sometimes the interview process went on for months, talking to this board member and that one. You begin to wonder if that's the way the whole organization runs.

From the time I got interested in nonprofits, it took about a year to actually start working. I started talking to the banks in January, sending out résumés and networking. The banks made offers by March or April. In November I got the offer from Enterprise, the microfinancing organization where I made my new career. During the search, I worked for two or three months with a Hartford nonprofit group that arranged environmental conferences for businesses to get a feel for it. Three days a week, I'd drive up there and help them out. That kept me going after I'd turned down the banks.

The hard work of making a career transition includes finding reason behind the emotions, digging deeper to understand our intuitions so we can use them as data, and, if still confused, crafting additional experiments. This is especially critical when we are using traditional routes, such as headhunters and outplacement centers, as well as the methods described here to take us to uncharted territory.

Committed Flirtation

Psychoanalyst Adam Phillips observes that "people tend to flirt only with serious things—madness, disaster, other people." [10] When we craft experiments, we are flirting with our many selves, a serious endeavor because it matters so much to us. The stronger the attraction, the more vulnerable we are to biases that affect how we perceive alternatives. Since we are not neutral about which outcome we prefer, we can fall into the trap of evaluating our experiments with a positive bias, one that encourages us to escalate commitment, even when we have evidence that it would be better to abandon ship or put the pet project on hold. [11] A related danger is inadvertently putting a current work situation at risk. The exploration feels risk free, because we hide it from work associates. But the project becomes all-consuming, and it becomes obvious to everyone around us that our attention is divided.

Mark Böllmer, a thirty-five-year-old Swiss manager working on a side project for a business in the area of socially responsible investment, gave himself one year to make a decision about leaving his corporate job. He started with a careful plan, outlining which benchmarks would tell him whether the business was worth pursuing. But, of course, we can never know what twists such projects will take, and he did not make any of his own benchmarks by his self-imposed December deadlines. By June of the following year, he was still working every spare moment to make his side project come to life.

After university, during his postgraduate engineering work at the prestigious École Polytechnique in Lausanne, Mark concentrated on environmental issues, going on to a local engineering firm to continue such work. There he wrote a guide to corporate environmental audits with a friend who eventually left to work in South America at an NGO. They worked day and night on that project, one of the most rewarding of his career. After three years and a desire for more hands-on experience, he moved to a large Swiss electricity company as the director of international projects, where, among other things, he started socially responsible projects in the field. But the managerial track he found himself on required him to move next into an operational role, which, since he worked for a large multinational firm, meant an expatriate assignment.

> *I'm in international projects, so the next step for me is to go into an operational role. The truth is, the idea of being a corporate guy at fifty just doesn't excite me. I'll pay the bulk of my salary in taxes and spend all my time involved in office politics. I'm not even sure I have what it takes to get to the top. I read in a study that the average age for starting a business in Switzerland is thirty-six. I'm thirty-five. I got married two years ago. We don't have children yet. I don't have a lot of constraints yet. It's now or never.*

When his coauthor on the environmental audits report returned to Lausanne, they decided to join forces and started working in their spare time to create a business linking corporate responsibility indices with company performance information. Following this strategy, they would be in the database management business.

> *The idea has evolved with work and market testing. We tried to form a relationship with a firm that would provide the data for the portal, but it wanted to distribute the information via existing online brokers and to hire me to do that work internally. That defeated our purpose. Now we're trying to create an asset-management company, through the development of funds. The dream is to become a real brand and to create a lucrative business. But I'm worried that as it moves more toward asset management, I'm getting further and further away from my area of expertise—international projects and environmental engineering.*

Experiments are inherently dangerous, though necessary. Like Mark, when we follow our passions, we also risk escalating our emotional commitment to a new course of action before we have evidence that it will be doable. On the other hand, the perpetual dilettante dabbles in a great variety of possibilities, like our would-be history professor, never committing to any and never crossing any off the list.

In between lies a stance of "committed flirtation," in which we hold ourselves to a rigorous search while withholding allegiance to any given alternative until the evidence that it will work is in. Ben's use of the experimental method is an example of committed flirtation. Starting with a "what if" question, Ben generated ideas and leads for possible avenues, testing and refining his developing notions about what he wanted to do next. It took several iterations, over a period of three years, to arrive at "the answer," but each step generated variety and feedback and suggested the next.

There is much we can do to adopt this experimental stance and adapt it to our own circumstances. In fact, probably the best barometer of our readiness to make change is whether we are willing and able to put a cherished possible self to the test. Leaping without a net is foolish. It is better to start by trying out a possible new role on a small scale—in our spare time, on a time-limited sabbatical, or as a weekend project. And as we will see in the next chapter, an added—and necessary—advantage of experimenting is that while we are trying out new roles, we meet people who will help change our lives.

shifting connections

W E CANNOT REGENERATE ourselves in isolation. We develop in and through our relationships with others—the master teaches the apprentice a new craft; the mentor guides a protégé through the passage to an inner circle; the council of peers monitors the standards of a professional group, conferring status within the community. Yet, when it comes to reinventing ourselves, the people who know us best are also the ones most likely to hinder rather than help. They may wish to be supportive but they tend to reinforce—or even desperately try to preserve—the old identities we are seeking to shed.

Changing careers is not merely a matter of changing the work we do. It is as much about changing the relationships that matter in our professional lives. *Shifting connections* refers to the practice of finding people who can help us see and grow into our new selves, people we admire, would like to emulate, and with whom we want to spend time. All reinventions require social support. But as this chapter reveals, it is hard to get the support we really need from career counselors, outplacers, or headhunters, or even from old friends, family members, or trusted colleagues. New or distant acquaintances—people and groups on the periphery of our existing networks—help us push off in new directions while providing the secure base in which change can take hold.

Harris's Story

After a four-week executive education program, Harris Roberts, thirty-nine, returned to his job ready for change. A regulatory affairs director at the health-care firm Pharmaco, Harris longed for bottom-line responsibility. He had advanced as much as he could as a staff person. His dream was to head one of the company's major divisions.

The executive program, a general management course for young high-potential managers, was part of a well-laid plan, concocted with the help of the firm's CEO, Alfred Mitchell, his long-term mentor. His promise to Harris was, "When you come back, we'll give you a business unit."

When Harris returned, a complicated new product introduction delayed the long-awaited transition. The CEO asked him to postpone his dream. He was needed. Instead of the top job, he was given a role as senior vice president, reporting to the division president, with responsibility for operations. Harris was disappointed. It was too much like what he had done before, and he was still not running anything.

But, always one to put the company first, he assented, after clearly and passionately reiterating his hopes and goals to his mentor. "There's no challenge anymore," he explained at the time.

> *Bring me any product and I can foresee the path it will take, the hurdles it will face, and how to best position it. I know I can make it work, whatever it is. I'm a good tactician. But I want to be a strategist. I want cross-functional experience so that I can move from executing a strategic plan formulated by someone else to being part of the team crafting the strategy.*

As insurance, he created for himself a network of mentors, all senior members of the firm, to watch over his development and help him find the next role.

It was a busy period. He had been the alumni coordinator for his executive program cohorts, the one charged with making sure they all stayed in touch. But as the pace picked up, Harris let his contacts fall by the wayside. Managing the approval of a radically new drug left him little time for extracurricular affairs. And the birth of his second child made it harder to squeeze in discretionary outside activities, like the conferences he liked to attend.

Headhunters had started to call after the executive program. Many health-care start-ups were seeking senior talent. People he admired left the company, including a close peer from the early days, Georgina James, who expressed to Harris her disillusionment with Pharmaco. "All my peers had already grown to the VP or presidential level," Georgina explained.

> We had created a new, creative, cutting-edge business. There were no road maps. We really built the division. I doubt whether I'll ever again experience such great years. But new people entered the equation. The firm became more structured, more political and bureaucratic. I had helped build the company, but I didn't know how to improve the bottom line anymore. My former boss went to a spin-off. His replacement didn't compare. Under his reign, no one grew.

As did many of his peers at Pharmaco, Harris entertained the idea of joining a late-stage start-up as a senior manager, potentially as CEO. But he fixated on what he perceived to be his shortcomings: finance and cross-functional experience. The executive program was supposed to round him out, but he still lacked confidence: "I didn't even know what the résumé of a small-firm CEO ought to look like." With a young family depending on him for a stable income, there were certain risks he wasn't prepared to take. When it came to the idea of his leaving a well-paid and secure post, his wife was the voice for stability.

Luckily, an unexpected turn of events allowed Harris to test his mettle as a general manager. His boss abruptly stepped down, leaving him to assume leadership of the business unit. They had butted heads about a restructuring plan for the organization, but now Harris was free to implement his own plan. Three months into his tenure as general manager, he was proud and confident. "It's going great," he reported.

I have taken full advantage of the opportunity to modify the business the way I believe necessary. So far, so good! I'm getting great support from the CEO and the board as well as from the rank and file. The people needed someone motivated to move the business forward and not simply to strip it down to a breakeven, as had been the game plan before. We are having frank, open discussions as never before. Wall Street seems to like it, too. We are focused, and the short-term financial results show it.

Unfortunately, almost as soon as he had attained control of the elusive bottom line, it was taken away from him. The corporation merged his business unit with another and acquired a third organization to absorb both within the parent. The head of the second unit, already executive vice president of Pharmaco, took the reins of the merged firm, leaving Harris once again without operational responsibility.

A little experience is a dangerous thing; by this point, even the way Harris talked about himself changed.

After a taste of running my own unit, I was not interested in running a product line. I wanted my own P&L [profit-and-loss statement]. The merger disrupted my grand plan: to learn to be a general manager in a nice, safe environment, within a corporate support structure, before moving out of the house. That didn't work out, but it helped me realize that I have the aptitude. I stopped worrying about not having all the skills because I saw I could learn them. I didn't doubt myself as I had before. Things had gone really well with me at the helm. Just realizing that the powers that be were wrong and I was right about how to restructure the company was a revelation. I learned to trust my intuition.

With his growing confidence, Harris also got serious about looking outside.

I started thinking more about expanding my contacts and my marketable assets. When I took a few minutes to think about outside networking, I realized that I had lost touch with some key individuals. I contacted two of those people and scheduled time to meet. Regarding the marketable assets, I began to think about what has made me successful in my career to date. It's not the regulatory expertise, which is what I had focused on earlier, but an approach to problem solving that made the regulatory piece work. So I asked myself, "How do you package such an abstract thing?"

Through Georgina James, who by then had left Pharmaco to become a health-care venture capitalist, Harris landed an offer to be the CEO of a Midwest technology start-up. He had no intention of tearing his family away from the Boston area, but it piqued his curiosity. He explored the offer thoroughly before turning it down. He also started going again to professional meetings. At one of those, he met Gerry Evans, the founder of a local health-care start-up and the inventor of a noncompeting product about which Evans needed regulatory advice. They developed an occasional relationship in which Gerry called on Harris for informal advice. Harris even took advantage of the time he spent at the gym to talk to others about what it's like to run a small business.

One day Harris took yet another call from Gerry. This time he wasn't calling for advice. Would Harris be his firm's COO and eventually assume the presidency?

He had heard about the merger and asked if we could discuss my future. When we met, he nailed me. He said, "I know you are a career Pharmaco person. I know that Alfred Mitchell is your mentor. I know you are seen as a star in the organization, that you are a valuable employee, and that there is a bright future there for you. I also know you have a young family. I know you are some-what risk averse because of the age of your kids and where you are in your career and what you want to do with your life."

I was blown away. These were not things I had ever told him. He had done his homework. He had called people who knew me within the industry. It allowed me to be very, very open with him, because he was right. His approach to me was, "I understand where your head is and there is no hurry. You take your time and you tell me what you need and there is no rush, because you are the guy we want. We want you with us running this company and making it a success."

By this time, I had been approached by a lot of people— by venture capitalists, by placement people—about CEO opportu-nities. I kept saying no, no, I'm not interested. I'm not really a good fit. I don't like the technology. I'm not going to live in Ohio. I was at a place in my career where I didn't have to leave; I could afford to be very picky about the opportunities. But I also started thinking to myself, "If I keep saying no, how many more times will I get asked to dance? When do people stop asking?" The size of the company was right, and the cash position was right. There was stability and the opportunity to be a key player and part of the strategy making about how to make it to the next level. I de-cided I was going to do it.

Ties That Bind (and Blind)

It wasn't just Harris's own lack of readiness that slowed his move. Early in the process, when pressed to explain why he didn't just look elsewhere, Harris acknowledged that he couldn't yet imagine leaving his firm. Thanks to a natural experiment during his three months at the helm of his division, he modified his perception that he was too weak in finance and cross-functional experience to be a good general manager. But to continue making progress toward his goal, he needed more than the growing confidence that comes with experience. He had to consider his social context, the web of contacts in which he was enmeshed.

Harris's problem was in part a lack of outside information. The demands of the immediate job, combined with family obligations, made it hard for him to keep his radar tuned to the marketplace. He didn't know what the CV of a small-firm CEO looked like because his knowledge was circumscribed by Pharmaco and the very regulatory circles he was trying to escape. Although he had vowed to stay in touch, after six months his network from the executive program had become inactive. He also lost contact with people who had "grown up" with him at Pharmaco but who had left the firm for greener pastures.

Yet an even more significant part of his resistance to change came from the people around him who were invested in his staying and who mirrored the view that he wasn't yet poised to take the leap. Harris had access to the power center of his firm. But his five mentors made not a gateway, but a fence that blocked the moves that would lead to career change. By talking only to people who inhabited his immediate professional world, who thought inside four walls about what opportunities he might move into, Harris seriously limited himself. Furthermore, those coworkers could no more let go of their ten-year-old image of Harris than he himself could. His story illustrates well just how much shifting connections is a necessary, though difficult, part of every career change.

In times of change and uncertainty, we take comfort in enduring ties with friends and family. Yet, as Robert Lifton writes, "These same sources of larger connectedness can be viewed as traps, as barriers to experimentation."[1] It is nearly impossible to change careers without altering our social and professional circles. To break the impasse, Harris had to distance himself from the core of his network while building up contacts at the periphery. Friends and coworkers had started to leave, creating, as he later realized, new sources for him to tap into. When the prize was taken from him a second time (with no substitute in sight), Harris got moving by contacting the people he used to know from Pharmaco.

In the mid-1970s, a Harvard sociologist named Mark Granovetter published what became the landmark study of how people get jobs.[2] What he found and others have confirmed, is still true today: Most people find their jobs through personal connections.[3] What surprised Granovetter—and hence the name of his famous "strength of weak ties" study—was that those personal contacts were neither friends, family, nor close work associates. They were distant acquaintances. Among those who got jobs through personal contacts, the great majority had interacted with that contact only occasionally or rarely.

Gary McCarthy, the would-be scuba diver turned Virgin capital-portfolio manager, illustrates this principle. He used his firm's network of alumni, calling people he once worked with as well as former MCG employees he didn't know. It was an ex-employee of his firm—a person he didn't know personally, but from whom he was two steps removed—who got him in the door at Virgin. Likewise, Harris's exit strategy came via a person he met casually at a professional conference, someone with whom he spoke no more than twice a year.

What makes a contact useful for a job change, argued Granovetter, is neither the closeness of our relationship with them nor the power of his or her position. It is the likelihood that the person knows different people than we do and, therefore, bumps into different information. The acquaintances, neighbors, and coworkers who operate in the same spheres as we do can rarely tell us something we don't already know because they hear about the same things we do. Of course, having an Ivy League, Oxbridge, or Grande École connection can dramatically improve one's prospects for moving into certain closed circles. But even members of elite tribes need "weak ties" to connect to worlds outside their immediate experience. Yet most people, like Harris, wait until they have been stuck for quite some time before starting to look outside their core circle of friends and colleagues.

Our close contacts don't just blind us, they also bind us to our outdated identities. Reinventing involves trying on and testing a variety of possible selves. But our long-standing social networks may resist those identity experiments. Remember Gary McCarthy's chagrin when he learned, three years out of college, that his family had already pegged him as a "finance person"? Without meaning to, friends and family pigeonhole us. Worse, they fear our changing.

In brainwashing studies—obviously one of the ultimate forms of identity change—standard operating practice is to separate subjects from all those who knew them previously, so as to deprive them of grounding in the old identity. Brainwashing tends to fail when subjects are allowed to return at night to their fellow prisoners (who knew them before) after a day of indoctrination.[4] We are all more malleable when separated from people who know us well. The same dynamic explains why young adults seem to change when they go away to college and interaction with family members and prior friends is necessarily reduced.

Of course, we don't need to subject ourselves to brainwashing in order to change careers. But we need to realize that our intimates—spouses, bosses, close friends, parents—expect us to remain the same, and they may pressure us to be consistent.[5] Most people who have made big career changes have heard loved ones tell them, "You're out of your mind." Sabotage is not their intention, but a shared history has entrenched certain expectations, and reinventing oneself can amount to breaking the implicit "contract." People who have quit smoking, lost weight, or gotten divorced are familiar with the mixed reactions of friends, who see the change as loss.

For Harris, the hardest thing about quitting Pharmaco was ending a long-term relationship with his mentor, the company's CEO, who saw Harris's leaving as a personal betrayal:

> *I had planned out my little speech. I said, "Alfred, I have really learned a lot from you, you've given me tons of opportunity. . . ." His reaction was worse than anything I imagined. He said, "I'm very disappointed. How can you do this to me after all I've done for you? I was grooming you for my job. Here I was training you to be a number 1 and you're going to go be a number 2. What are*

you doing to the organization?" By the time his tirade was over, I felt like a wet rag. I really love the company and he's like my father. His disapproval was hard to bear.

Pragmatically, a career change requires weak-tie contacts outside the daily grind to provide leads, referrals, job information, and entrées to organizations and decision makers. And, emotionally, it is hard to get validation for a new self without making shifts in our social relationships. When change entails rethinking our very identity, we need substitutes for the people and groups we have to leave behind and role models for whom we might become.

New Faces, New Places

In the difficult days of the in-between period, a desire to move on must be coupled with a drive to find strength, wisdom, and emotional support, if only on the outer boundaries of our social world. The practice of shifting connections, as we describe in more detail below, entails looking for new peer groups, guiding figures, and communities of practice. Psychologically, a process of identification is at work: As we encounter people whom we see as sharing something fundamental with us, even if only in our aspirations, we flesh out our ideas (and ideals) of what we are becoming. Consider how many times we have heard people reproach their organizations by saying, "There is no one there I want to be like." The reinventing process corrects this deficiency, heightening our desire for role models and people we can relate to. These people and groups provide a "safe base" that enables us to take risks with our new selves and a professional community in which we can develop a new sense of belonging.

New Peer Groups

Even before Harris started to look for work outside his firm, he began to shift his point of reference to a new peer group. His boss left for a start-up, followed by a highly regarded peer, Georgina. On the heels of her departure, he attended an alumni reunion event where he met others who had successfully changed careers. It seemed like everyone was changing but him. Much like the participants in the "becoming an ex" study described in chapter 3, Harris began to identify with the values, norms, attitudes, and expectations of entrepreneurs and small-business people. As he sought out those who had already left Pharmaco and saw them accomplishing things they would not previously have imagined, his confidence and resolve were bolstered.

The same occurred for Julio Gonzales, a forty-three-year-old heart surgeon. When Julio started a one-year midcareer course at a public-policy school, he shifted his reference group from medical coworkers at his old job to fellow students and professors. He felt a greater kinship with the latter, and the new relationships that formed became doorways to new worlds for him. His new peers led Julio to realize that he was not a "mutant" for wanting to change; in fact, he became increasingly comfortable with his new affinities. New peer groups might consist of people who are experiencing similar doubts about old paths (e.g., fellow students in a midcareer course) or who are already doing the new (e.g., the small-business entrepreneurs Harris started seeking out). What matters, psychologically, is that we come to feel that important characteristics that define them also define us.

As our points of comparison shift from inside to outside our organization, and as we encounter more and more people who have changed careers, a "tipping point" occurs.[6] Our actions become self-reinforcing: We start to feel more determined to make a change and seek out others who have already done so. Seeing their success makes us doubly determined to make a change, and we take other actions that in turn tip the scales in favor of change. Leif Hagstrom, who went back to school before taking the leap from a large Norwegian bank to a New York travel start-up, for example, sought out among his fellow students those who wanted to make a change. From them, he gained validation for his feelings. In the same way that after we buy a new automobile, we notice how many other people have the same car, once we have decided to change, we look for information that confirms our emerging beliefs (and ignore evidence that might disconfirm our point of view).[7]

Guiding Figures

Yale psychologist Daniel Levinson, whose book *The Seasons of a Man's Life* explained the midlife crisis, emphasized the importance of guiding figures: people from whom the person in transition gets encouragement and learns new ways to live and work.[8] Guiding figures help us to endure the ambiguity of the in-between period by conferring blessings, believing in our dreams, and creating safe spaces within which we can imagine and try out possibilities. More than a contact who opens a door or offers a job lead, the guiding figure is special because of his or her connection to our dream of the life we want to move into. The "dream" as Levinson describes it is much like a favorite possible self: "It has the quality of a vision, and imagined possibility that generates excitement and vitality. At the start it is poorly articulated and only tenuously connected to reality."[9] The guiding figure embodies that possibility and shapes it through his or her efforts as teacher, critic, sponsor, or mentor. In Gerry Evans, Harris found a person who not only believed in his potential as a general manager but who also offered him the kind of close and interdependent working relationship he had never had before and now was ready for.

> *It was such a contrast to my relationship with Alfred. It's not as paternal. Gerry knows things I need to learn—things that relate to creative financing, ways to raise money—but he also needs to learn from me. He doesn't know how to run a company, and I do. He's looking to me to teach him what's necessary to develop an organization, to build a foundation. I think I can learn a lot from Gerry, but it's a more mature and more professional relationship than I had with Alfred.*

Another important role a guiding figure plays is to reassure us that we are not out of our minds, to convey that what we are contemplating is not only reasonable but totally consistent with a wise assessment of our potential. The counsel of an elder is also essential because the person in transition cannot see what lies over the horizon: "He needs guidance not merely because in the conventional sense he needs someone to teach him skills, but because some very surprising things are happening to him that require explanation," writes sociologist Anselm L. Strauss in his seminal work on the search for identity, "because the sequence of steps are in some measure obscure, and because one's own responses become something out of the ordinary, someone must stand prepared to predict, indicate, and explain the signs."[10]

Ben Forrester, who shifted from academia to nonprofit consulting, relied on a former boss, Tim Turner, to step in and help him make sense of what was happening to him. The work he was doing required new skills, and the way people worked together was also new and unfamiliar.

> *As managing partner, I am charged with both setting direction for the organization and ensuring the full engagement of the other partners. It can be challenging trying to sort out those two roles—and it is certainly different than being a professor. The style, pace, and cycle time are not at all the same. When you go out to make a pitch, you can't be ambivalent about why they should give you a lot of money. In academia, you are supposed to be a dispassionate observer, but now I have to be a strong advocate. And the feedback is immediate. You know right away: They say yes or no to a fund-raising pitch, as opposed to waiting a year to get a reviewer's comments on an academic article.*

Tim reassured Ben that the challenges he was experiencing were normal, that he had once felt those things too, and that it simply was part of the reality of leading a group of professionals.

> *Tim has great insight. He'll say, "I know what you're feeling. That's what I live with every day. My job is to maximize everyone's productivity." Or, when he sees me getting frustrated, he'll say, "This is an exercise in character building." When I find myself in an ego*

*battle, I ask myself, "Does this matter?" His coaching has helped
me a lot because I'm trying to figure out what is the right model of
"leadership" in the professional world. It can't be run like a conventional business because partners won't be told what to do.
They won't "work for someone."*

Having a mentor in Tim was validation for the new but still
tentative identity Ben was constructing as a leader of a nonprofit
consulting organization.

Since future steps are so unclear to the person who is changing, a guiding figure can also be a reality check. As Julio Gonzales
considered alternatives to a medical career, his leadership professor (who was also a psychiatrist) was particularly important, both
as a role model for the kind of work Julio dreamed of doing one
day and as a valued source of advice for managing the transition.
He helped Julio set more realistic expectations and take the edge
off the next job decision, telling him,

*You're not going to figure this out this year. A year is not long
enough. You're going to have to consider doing something on the
way to something else. So don't get obsessed about making the
right decision. Make a plan to tide you over for the next three
years until you figure out the longer-term plan.*

Julio's guide also broke it to him that there would be no easy
answers. Says Julio,

*My plan was, O.K., I can't figure it out, but I'm going to step
back and take a year off at great financial risk. And then one
night at 3:00 in the morning I'm going to be woken up and there's
going to be a star and I'm going to know what to do. I wanted
somebody to tell me, "This is what you've got to do, and it will
be all right." My professor helped me see my naïveté.*

Where does one find such a guide? In many cases, it is a simple
matter of serendipity. Pierre Gerard was invited to a dinner with

the Buddhist monk who became his guide; Lucy Hartman's group brought in the organizational development coach who became her own coach and role model. But from there, it was up to them to recognize the potential and pursue the relationship. Gary McCarthy and June Prescott made finding people who might take them on as apprentices their explicit transition goals: Gary made a list of entrepreneurs he admired and set out to network his way into their organizations; June wrote to a columnist whose writing she admired, asking him to meet and advise her.

Although a person with whom we have had a long-standing connection can be a guide, he or she is seldom someone we have been seeing regularly. It might be an old boss (like Ben's) or a school friend we lost sight of; often guides are completely new contacts (like Harris's), with whom we feel free to try out new personas without violating anyone's expectations. Whatever the original relationship, the strong bond that develops between the person in transition and the guiding figure creates a safe zone within which the change idea starts becoming a real possibility. A necessary feature of this relationship is that it develops outside the web of routine professional interactions in which the person has been embedded (and may be trying to break out of).

Communities of Practice

The term "communities of practice" was coined to describe a kind of social participation that is crucial for "learning to be."[11] The argument is that learning any line of work is a social process in which we become active participants in the practices of a social community, constructing new identities in relation to this community and its members. Apprentices do not learn a craft by going to school to learn abstract, textbook knowledge; rather, they learn to function as a part of a community in which their initial participation is legitimate but peripheral. We change careers in the same way.

William Bridges, the best-selling author of the book *Transitions*, was a professor of English for twelve years before he became a consultant, lecturer, and writer on topics related to personal development. By his own account, it took him several years of experimenting to define a next career. Not surprisingly, Bridge's intimate circle did not encourage him to explore alternatives. His friends and family were voices for stability. Bridges started building his escape route by way of small experiments. But what really allowed him to make the break was the community of practice that became his new home base.

"It took me a couple of years to work up my courage to leave teaching," he stated in an interview with management thinker Tom Peters.[12]

> *And then it took me two or three years of experimenting after I had done so to find a path that was a real replacement. It was a five-year process. My experiments started when I was still teaching. I pushed literature courses farther and farther away from literature and toward self-exploration. I, for example, taught a course in autobiography. Which really was a pure and simple excuse for having people search their own lives to find a path for themselves, where they were going. That was one exploration. But I was scared to leave teaching, so I pushed the boundaries of what I was doing as far as I dared.*
>
> *The actual crossover point came rather serendipitously. I got involved with a group of people who were starting a counseling center in Palo Alto and I got in the training program for lay therapists. There was an experiment to have nonprofessionals actually trained as therapists and to do therapy under the direction of a therapist. I was doing this in my after-hours life. It was very exciting. There were six families in which one or the other partner was in the training program. We were meeting together after these training sessions; we really liked each other. And we talked about living closer together and so on and the upshot of it was that we decided to form an "intentional community." Not a commune, in one house, but a community.*
>
> *We started looking for property and finally found eighty acres near the Russian River in California. This thing which had*

nothing to do with my original purposes for leaving teaching was the precipitating event that finally got me to quit. Mills College, where I'd been teaching, was too far away. I couldn't keep teaching. I didn't really want to anyway, but I used that as an excuse to make the break. . . . I came from a long line of teachers and the idea of leaving not only a tenured position, which I had, an endowed professorship, was scary. . . . These voices in my head, which were largely, I think, family voices, said, "This is insane, this is crazy. What is it you're going to do?" Of course I didn't have an answer yet. . . . This dialogue was going on in my head and I think finding this community group really helped me.

Just like guiding figures, new communities play a number of important roles: They offer inclusion, provide a safe base, and replace the community that is being lost. Communities of practice are an integral part of the test-and-learn method because we need a context in which to learn both the substance and style of the new self we are trying to become. Some of us, like Ben Forrester, are lucky enough to find a guiding figure who can also teach us the tacit knowledge of the occupation we are trying to enter; more often than not, however, we have to learn by doing and participating in whatever limited way we can in the life of the group we'd like to join.

Consider how a person moves into a career the first time around, as a young adult. Apprentices work with their mentors and learn craftsmanship by observation, imitation, and practice. Newcomers to a profession or organization are socialized by old-timers, meaning that they are taught not only the required skills and rules but also how to acquire the right look and feel—the social norms that govern how they should conduct themselves so as to become true members.[13] In the same way, reinventing oneself as a member of a new occupational world is a process of becoming an insider to that world, learning its subjective viewpoint, language, demeanor, and outlook. But since apprenticeships and internships typically exist in institutional form for only the young, at midcareer we are left to our own devices when it comes to picking up the tacit knowledge of the new work we wish to do. It is up to us to create or find our own community.

If we are free to try out any identity we like, it is also true that we must rely on others to complete the picture of which we are only allowed to paint certain parts.[14] The desired identity remains incomplete and tentative without the stamp of approval of a new peer group, mentor, or community. It is important to conduct our "role rehearsals" outside our usual circles because the old audience tends to narrowly typecast us.

A Secure Base

All transformation processes, in nature as in society, require a protected space for change—the cocoon, the chrysalis, the womb, the make-believe space, the apprenticeship, or the internship. Making a career transition likewise requires psychological safety.[15] To come up with a creative solution for a next career, we have to be able to test unformed, even risky, identities in a relatively safe and secure environment, an incubator of sorts in which premature identities can be nurtured until a viable possibility emerges. Relationships create such an environment.

In the 1950s, psychologists showed that baby animals could become so highly attached to mother substitutes like brooms and wire figures that they would ignore their actual mothers. Such studies formed the foundation of a more general theory about the sort of human attachment that is critical for any risk taking.[16] These "imprinting" studies pointed to the paradoxical nature of self-reliance and paved the way for the notion that people, like baby monkeys, are only capable of being fully self-reliant when they feel supported by and attached to trusted others. In making a career change, we are breaking attachments that no longer work for us, while building new connections that can support us through the transition.

Many of our ideas about psychological safety derive from research on the stages of maturity and predictable transition periods that children go through. Children imagine various possibilities for themselves in the future, and they play out those possibilities via games, reverie, and make-believe explorations. The play world they create demarcates a region between an objective external reality and the entirely subjective internal world in which the child prepares for the hard work of making the illusions real in the external world.[17] The role of the mother is to provide a safety zone in which the child can give rein to his or her imagination. In that space, the child feels protected, safe from any danger. He or she can gradually define and test out a newly emerging self, with the mother's blessing.

What kind of adult relationship provides such psychological safety? In developmental theory, a "good-enough mother" neither stifles nor ignores the child, neither intrudes nor abandons, but rather gives the child enough rope for discovery, all the while conveying that she is nearby if needed. Likewise, a guiding figure is neither unresponsive when we need help while in transition nor overprotective when we need to operate and explore on our own. Harris's old mentor was unable to assume this role—he could give Harris neither enough room to experiment with a general management role nor close enough counsel on how to get there. In adulthood, therefore, a guiding figure also helps us get to the next stage by creating a safety zone in which we can create, experiment with, and slowly actualize the new self just starting to take shape.

Like the child taking his or her first steps, the person trying to make a career change will find it difficult to take risks if he or she is preoccupied with psychological safety and security. People of all ages are happiest and best able to deploy their talents when they are confident that, standing behind them, there are one or more trusted persons who will come to their aid should difficulties arise.[18] We need a secure base from which to operate. But there is an added twist when it comes to career change: The necessary secure base cannot be close to home.

Throughout this chapter, we have seen that the only way to make a true career change is by shifting connections from the core to the periphery of our networks—finding new peer groups with whom to compare ourselves, looking for guiding figures to encourage us, and joining new communities of practice. The contacts that bring us new ideas and possibilities are not always immediate sources of comfort and reassurance. We must also venture into unknown networks—and not just for job leads. Making a significant change requires more than a little help from our new friends, mentors, guides, and role models. As we'll see in the following chapter, often it is strangers who help us make sense of where we are going and who we will become.

making sense

I N THE MIDDLE of confusion, many of us hope for one event that will clarify everything, that will transform our stumbling moves into a story that makes sense. Julio Gonzales, a doctor trying to leave the practice of medicine, put it like this: "I was waiting for an epiphany. I wake up in the middle of the night and the Angel of Mercy tells me *this* is what I should do." Some people do experience pivotal moments in which what they are seeking is crystallized. But for every person who changes career in response to some sort of trigger, another fails to take the leap, and a third finds a moment of truth in a trivial but symbolic occurrence.

Making sense refers to the practice of putting a frame around experience: interpreting what is happening today, reinterpreting past events, and creating compelling stories that link the two.[1] A life story defines us. Consider how we come to feel that we really know someone: We might know them well enough to predict their behavior; but we only really know them when we know their stories—the underlying narratives that lend meaning, unity, and purpose to their lives.[2] The same is true for knowing ourselves. As this chapter illustrates, we make sense of chaotic changes by infusing events with special meaning and weaving them into coherent stories about who we are becoming.

John's Story

John Alexander, a forty-four-year-old British investment banker, decided to put aside his skepticism when a friend urged him to go see an astrologer. He expected a generic prognosis. To his surprise, the first thing she said to him was, "I'm glad I haven't been you for the last two or three years. You have been undergoing a painful internal tug-of-war between two opposing factions. One side wants stability, economic well-being, and social status, and the other craves artistic expression, maybe as a writer or an impresario. You may wish to believe that there can be reconciliation between these two. I tell you, there cannot be."

Around his fortieth birthday, John had given himself two years to devise a way out of a successful but unsatisfying career in the City, London's financial district.

In fact, it took me five years. I think when you're going for a complete change, it takes longer than you guess. All I knew to begin with was that I didn't like being a banker. There is something rather empty about finance. It's glossy. It's interesting. Sometimes, there are really good moments. And clearly you're well paid. But most bankers do not feel, at the heart of it, that they're doing something worthwhile. I was becoming increasingly uncomfortable as my role shifted from being a client's trusted adviser to being a salesman pushing the deal. I hated having to admit at a party that I was an investment banker. I would go to intense lengths to try to avoid it.

To tell the truth, I never felt comfortable in my own skin in the City. I was recruited to banking out of the foreign service, where over lunch you might talk about archeology or butterflies or Chinese ceramics—we were conversant in a whole range of subjects. I remember the first day I went to the Buren's canteen. All people could talk about, in some form or another, was money. In fifteen years, I never went back.

But the reason I wanted out, really, was much more fundamental. I just believed that if I stayed there until, say, age fifty-five, and then put my feet up for five years and then at age sixty looked back on what I'd done, I would not feel that I had made the most of my one unrepeatable life. So I decided I had to get out.

At first I went through the fairly routine areas former bankers enter: How about something like venture capital? Could I get a fund together? Could I form a team to buy some company, improve it, then sell it? I concluded that that was just the same thing dressed in different clothes. I would just be deferring a problem, not solving it, and it would not get easier to solve. I urgently felt the need to change sooner rather than later.

But I utterly rejected the thought of looking for just any new job. I had figured out by then that I didn't want to be part of an organization, that I'd come to dislike everything that went with a big one—not the work per se, but the interminable meetings, the constant e-mail junk, and all the other busywork. Another thing that put me off it was the increasingly political nature of those places. One year, you can be the guy that everybody wants to have on every committee, your star is on the rise, and then six months later, nobody wants to say hello. I'm not a political animal, and I didn't want to try to become one.

It is hard to say when I started wanting to write. Many years ago, on vacation, I fooled around with writing a novel, but I never intended to publish it. I never gave it another thought. Writing is something you're encouraged to perfect in the foreign service, and I had a natural aptitude. So when I decided I would change careers, it seemed a promising possibility.

I started by asking myself how I could take natural interests and convert them into a career. I established a link with two small companies, a car retailer and hi-fi company that I patronized. I became an unpaid consultant and have remained so. In my darkest hours of banking, I took solace from ringing them up and just chatting about what was going on in their worlds. It was quite a good way for me to learn what it felt like to work with them, to understand their pressures, their cash flow problems, their staff problems.

By the time I found myself in front of this astrologer, I had already had three to four years of explaining my predicament to friends and family. It was always, "On the one hand this, on the other that," with no clear view emerging. They would tend to say, "I can see why writing might be interesting, but you've got a very good job and do you really want to jeopardize that?" All their advice had just added up to a fog.

Then, suddenly here was this astrologer who after ninety seconds said, "This is mortal combat. The one that will win is. . . ." She probably didn't pause at all, but it felt like one of those moments when time freezes. I had clarity after four years of fog. Before she said the next word, suddenly a voice on my shoulder was saying, "Oh please, let it be the artistic side," knowing that if she said, "By the way, it's the other one," I would have died a little. Anyway, she said, "The answer is the artistic side."

After forty-five minutes, we stopped the astrology and just talked. I admitted my true situation, including the fact that I would like to write a book. I talked about my earlier, nonserious attempt at writing and after about three minutes, she said, "Stop, I can't stand this. I wish you could hear yourself. You are saying, if I have an idea for a book, which is most unlikely, even if I get a good idea, I'll probably never get around to starting it, and if I do, obviously I'll never finish it. If I do, of course it will never get published, even in the wildest chance that it got published, of course it will be unsuccessful. What are you doing? You're trying to protect yourself from failure, and it won't work."

This session was, by far, the most significant hour of my life. I left her house and went for a little walk in a public park. I devised two questions for myself there and then. It's so simple that it's ludicrous, but my God, it worked for me. I was forty-four. I fast-forwarded to an age at which I thought, fundamentally, it's all over. I picked seventy-five. My first question, starting from the vantage point of the seventy-five-year-old looking back at the forty-four-year-old, was, "If the forty-four-year-old identified something that he really wanted to do and it was really risky and he tried it and he failed—possibly fell on his face very publicly, with dire economic consequences—can the seventy-five-year-old cope with that?"

The answer was, "Yes, as long as the forty-four-year-old gave it his best shot." And I then said, "OK, next question. Same vantage point, same younger guy. Let's assume the forty-four-year-old knew what he wanted to do, had identified it, but decided that the risk for social failure and economic failure was just too great and therefore never did it. How would the seventy-five-year-old feel about that?" And I thought that would be unforgivable. Next, a very weird thing happened to me: It was almost a physical sensation. At that instant, I lost the fear of failure, and it has never come back. It was like losing vertigo. By the way, I am not indifferent to failure. I worried about what people would think and what would happen if I failed.

John did all the research for his first book, a financial-world thriller, in his spare time, then scraped together every possible bit of vacation time to go away and write it. By the time he left the bank a year later, the novel was finished, and he had a contract to publish it. Before quitting, he also sold the film rights to Universal.

Novel writing has become the core of John's new work life, which comprises a portfolio of different professional activities. A second ring is running Masterprize, an international competition for contemporary composers that he created and convinced the BBC and EMI to sponsor. Founding a boutique investment bank, the third ring, was not part of the plan.

I had expected to leave banking-related things altogether. But three of my clients who were big companies said to me independently that they would like to keep in touch. Could I find a way to make that possible? I said, "I have no brand, no machine." And they said, "We don't care about stuff like that. What we appreciate is honest advice, and we always trusted you." And I learned that giving advice to people who have already decided what they want is really quite enjoyable, provided it didn't get in the way of the books and the music. The bit I disliked was having to go into that bank every morning.

In the end John settled on a portfolio career, pursuing a varied mix of different ventures, some for pay, some as gift work; some that exploit his past experience, some that let him explore new frontiers.[3] Recognizing that managing any diverse portfolio is a long-term gambit, he concludes:

You have to be willing to say I am actually going to invest in growing a new life, where I am supporting things I really love, where I can meet interesting people, whether they are painters, musicians and dancers, or people who have my accounts. I want to get involved, not just with my money. I want to have a part to play as well.

Alert Intermissions

In an essay about how we change our opinions, novelist Nicholson Baker argues that most of the time, we are in some inconclusive phase of changing our minds about many things, without being consciously aware that we are doing so. Events intrude and interrupt, occasioning what he calls *alert intermissions*.[4] Many stories of career change, like John's, tell about such alert intermissions—moments when pivotal events catalyze change.

All of us hope for those moments and mistake them for coincidences or rare occurrences. In fact, we create alert intermissions. For starters, we pay attention to things that justify what we want to do. An event that is rated insignificant by one person can be infused with meaning for another. During a career transition, our sense of identity is fluid and shifting, and so are the frames we apply to our experience. People, places, and things that might have gone unnoticed before become significant if they serve the cause of our reinvention.

Alert intermissions test and shape our possible selves.[5] They clarify possibilities by offering sharper, more vivid and concentrated versions of what we have been sensing day to day. By the time John went to see the astrologer, he knew he wanted to write; most certainly, there had been other moments—plenty of them—that might have revealed his creative side. Perhaps the consultation with the astrologer stood out because it also disclosed the battle of identities that was at the heart of his paralysis. Alert intermissions make us aware of forks in the road; they force us to choose one possible self over another. John's episode identified the creative possible self as his favorite, crystallizing a compelling image of himself that was still in the formative stage. The writer in him, in turn, became a beacon for future choices.

Unexpected events often provoke insights that allow progress toward a solution after a period of being stuck.[6] They allow us to reframe our stories. For John, the revelation was not that he should become a writer. It was that he could not live in two worlds and that he would have to come to terms with letting go of the old identity that was slowing him down. John had never stopped to challenge his basic assumption that he could maintain his old social and financial status while moving into a realm that would allow him greater artistic expression. The astrologer told him he had to choose. It had a big impact not because she revealed something he did not know (if that were the case, she could not have catalyzed a change) but because all the experiences he had been having suddenly made sense in this new light. That encounter lent coherence to all the bits of knowledge, information, and feelings he had yet to put together.

Events can have these crystallizing effects because they intrude and interrupt our daily routine, forcing us to step back. An active person by nature, John had filled every waking moment with his search for an escape route. The astrologer episode made him slow down, provoking the walk in the park in which he stepped back from his frenetic search to question what he really wanted in life. John's insight did not come to him at work nor did it come during a particularly busy period. Moments of insight—the culmination of meaning in a brief time span—tend to occur when we change contexts, when we are relaxed, when we put aside our problem for a while, or when we are doing something out of character—in John's case, going to an astrologer.

But such insights on their own cannot drive a career transition to its culmination. They have to be worked into a compelling story. Why? Because we define who we are by our life stories. And stories about change, by definition, require a "before" and "after." Events are merely occasions for retelling, reworking, and reassembling our experiences. We are literally reinventing the past so that it flows into a future we desire. In John's case, the astrologer episode gave him a dramatic moment around which he could construct a story that would explain his actions as he left the bank. Knowing the story gave him motivation and purpose.

Our stories are not only for private consumption. They also help others make sense of what may seem like nonsensical actions, such as quitting a prestigious job instead of hanging on for early retirement. Without a good story, it is harder to get others to help us change. Certainly John's encounter with the astrologer had a dramatic quality, but he dramatized it further for his own purposes, to signal to himself and others that the time had come to make a change.

One of the most interesting things about reinvention stories is how much they change along the way. Since a good story is defined by a narrative structure—a beginning, a low point, a climax, and an ending—the end point helps determine the beginning and the low point.[7] Knowing the end point tells us which events are relevant. For example, John's experience in the bank's canteen on his first day at work becomes telling in the context of his leaving the bank to do the very things he could not share with the peers he joined for lunch that day. Since we need to know the end point in order to craft a good story, alert intermissions tend to come late in the transition process.

Only when the end is in sight can we recognize a turning point. John's defining moment came at age forty-four, four full years after he had been working at finding a way out. As Nicholson Baker writes, "We must not overlook sudden conversions and wrenching insights, but usually we fasten onto these only in hindsight, and exaggerate them for the sake of the narrative."[8] The truth is that, for John, insight came to a mind prepared by a period of what he described as very, very hard work to come up with alternatives to his banking career. As we explore below, the practice of making sense consists of three parts: taking advantage of the events of our lives to reconsider our selves, stepping back periodically to allow insight to jell, and using both the events and our interpretations of them to work and rework our story.

Defining Moments

Arranging life's events into a coherent story is one of the most subtle yet demanding challenges of career reinvention. To reinvent oneself is to rework one's story, revising it frequently, trying out different versions on others. Events punctuate continuous experience, giving us some pegs on which to hang our reinvention stories. Some events unfreeze us, help us start moving away from the old; other events focus our energies toward the future, helping the new direction to jell.

As a thirty-nine-year-old general manager at a large New York publishing house, Brenda Rayport attended a convention of economists to promote one of her books.

We had hired a caricaturist to draw cartoons of the professors whose textbooks we sold, and he offered to do a caricature of me. His technique was to ask people about their hobbies and interests. He would draw the figures with their little emblems around them. I thought, what will he depict in his drawing of me? A textbook? I didn't have anything else in my life at that point. My marriage was no good. I didn't have any hobbies. I said to myself,

"I'm passionate about my work, but is this what I want arrayed in the caricature of myself that I'll hang in my office? I don't think so." It really bothered me. For the three or four weeks leading up to the conference, I was sweating about what he was going to draw around me. It became clear that I was doing something very wrong in my life.

A major change in her company's internal management (one she did not like), a new "commuter" relationship, and a looming fortieth birthday were bits and pieces already nudging Brenda to reexamine her fifteen-year career in publishing. The cartoon episode made it all click in a way that started her moving. Anticipating her caricature became a pivotal moment for Brenda.

I graduated from college in 1980 with a liberal arts degree, and I knew I wanted a career in publishing. So I went into educational publishing at Addison-Wesley, which offered a career track and a kind of professionalism. I started in sales. That meant that I lived in a small town; had a home office, a book bag, and a company car; and called on instructors. Then I moved to New York to work as an editor, starting out in engineering. Eventually, I became editor-in-chief of that group, which generated about $7 million in annual revenues. I was starting to think about what might come next when my boss, out of the blue, asked me to take over as head of the English as a second language division, which needed a turnaround. Its revenues started at $14 million a year from sales channels and product lines all across the world. It had grown at about 2 percent for five years. I mean, it was a real backwater. This prompted not only a move to New York but also a divorce, which was long in coming anyway. At the end of three years, my division was worth $40 million and had become a model for the company. Managing that kind of growth was really, really, really fun.

But the mergers and acquisitions of that period led to enormous changes. People were coming and going, and I started to feel how little power I had, even as a pretty successful general manager. I was a considered a star, but I had a small division and not a lot of clout. I started seeing how dependent I was on top-level managers, for whom I was just a pawn, and I saw that my people were just pawns. There was no way of knowing whether the game being played now would be the game played six months later. The board shifted twice a year. That angered me because real people and real results were riding on the board. I was effective politically, negotiating the interests of my division, but I didn't like having to focus on the internal dynamics of the company rather than the external dynamics of the market.

And then there was a personal shift. I met my future husband, Aaron, who lived in Chicago. As a general manager, I had completely given up any personal life. I was totally career oriented. I loved my job, but I couldn't imagine doing it and having a full life. The business was global, I was on the road two weeks out of four the whole year round, I don't think I spent a Memorial Day or July 4th or a Labor Day at home for four years. Suddenly I was getting married again, and Aaron and I had to decide how to put our lives and careers together. I moved to Chicago determined to be a whole person again, which meant having to develop those parts of me that were quite underdeveloped. I was going to make damn sure that the next time someone had to draw a picture of me, there would be plenty of things to put around it.

It took Brenda close to three years after the cartoon episode to figure out a new direction. In the interim, the episode became a guiding image she used each time she came to a fork in a road, to remind herself of the feared possible self she was still at risk of reverting to, and its counterpart, the still vague but much desired Brenda with a multifaceted, rich life.

All reinvention stories, like Brenda's and John's, have defining moments. As we will explore with other examples below, some of these moments can be dramatic, like John's, and lead to seemingly abrupt shifts. Others, like Brenda's, are symbolic, small events that gradually shape a whole series of career and life decisions. Some, like Brenda's, come relatively early in the transition process, unfreezing her and jump-starting change. Others, like John's, come a bit later and help a new idea to coalesce. Defining moments make it clear that there is no turning back. They tell us that old lines of work have run their course and failed, been irrevocably disrupted, or simply do not satisfy us anymore. They signal that we are ripe for action, make us more attentive to new ideas, and trumpet our readiness to those around us.

Unfreezing Events

Early transition events unfreeze us—get us unstuck, ready to move—by making more vivid a feared possible self. Our early doubts about our current career may seem too vague and nonspecific to justify action; but after a defining event, we have concrete evidence of a problem. In Brenda's case, the cartoon episode showed that her life as an executive was exacting a higher cost than she realized. The event unfreezes by challenging a strongly held or cherished self-conception, such as Brenda's belief that she was a dynamic person with broad interests. That self-conception was shattered the moment she could not think of what might be drawn around her. Getting fired and receiving a bad performance review are classic unfreezing events. Events like these defy the view of ourselves as competent professionals; they can make us realize we are *not* in the driver's seat when it comes to career decisions and bring our feared possible selves more sharply into focus.

Of course, the event by itself is insufficient for sparking change; we can always ignore the information; dismiss it as irrelevant; blame the undesired outcome on fate; or, most common, simply deny its validity.[9] But, when we are ready (and as we'll see below, readiness is only a matter of hard work and preparation), events develop self-awareness. Early philosophers argued that we cannot perceive our selves directly, rather our selves must be "caught in the act" of perceiving something that exists in the real world.[10] Self-knowledge, therefore, comes from our reactions to things that happen to us and around us. Just as we learn about other people by observing their behavior and making inferences from it, we learn about our selves by examining what we do when events force our hand—yet another reason why solitary introspection is insufficient and why experimenting provides more useful information than reflecting on past experience.

One of the primary ways in which unfreezing events mark a cut with the past and herald the start of a transition period, according to psychoanalyst Manfred Kets de Vries, is by serving as an organizing scheme for everything that occurs afterwards: "From this point on, every new disturbance is recognized as part of the same pattern of dissatisfaction," he writes.

> *Complaints coalesce into a coherent entity. Many people have an "aha" experience at this stage, a moment when they are finally able to interpret decisively what is happening to them. They see clearly that neither the passage of time nor minor changes in behavior will improve the situation—indeed the situation is likely to become even worse if nothing drastic is done about it. Even the insight that drastic measures are required does not automatically compel people to take action. However, it typically sets into motion a mental process whereby they consider alternatives to the adverse situation."* [11]

Unfreezing events may be either happy or sad. People in transition often tell stories of jolts and losses in their personal lives that remind them of ignored possible selves or warn them of the harmful consequences of current identities. But joyful events like births or marriages can also be occasions for revising priorities. Events that mark the passage of time, such as a milestone birthday, a tenth anniversary, or an alumni reunion, can also unfreeze us. Likewise, a natural conclusion to a project or the time when a particular role comes to an end can start our juices flowing. Just as being passed over for a promotion can be a trigger, a new assignment might cause people to see more clearly that they no longer desire the future they were inexorably moving toward.

Jelling Events

In almost every story of career change come to fruition, there is a palpable moment when things click into place, as they did for John Alexander. A new option materializes. Taking the leap looks easy. Diverse experiences form an intelligible pattern; feelings that had been building up jell as a coherent story. Facts and intuitions, reason and emotion come together, and we feel ready to seize the moment. These moments of crystallization tend to occur much later in the transition; most often they are an effect, rather than a cause of, change.

Harris Roberts had such a moment *after* he announced his resignation as a regulatory expert at Pharmaco. Having gathered his courage to confront his mentor with the news, Harris was wracked with doubt about his decision and even began to second-guess himself when he absorbed Alfred's reaction. Then came a moment when it all made sense.

> *After I talked to Alfred, I picked up a book of poems that a friend had given me. I'd had it for a while but hadn't gotten around to reading it. The very first poem is about leaving. I don't remember the exact words, but it says something like, "You're leaving your house, there's wind, there's darkness and you start hearing people's voices and they say, mend my life, don't go, don't go, mend my life." And I thought, Wow! Slap me in the head. If I stayed, why would I be staying? I would stay for them, not for me. I would be staying because Alfred Mitchell said, "You can't do this to me." That's when I realized that this was like a bad marriage. That's when it became clear to me why I was leaving. I wasn't, and maybe never would be, participating in defining the structure and future of the organization. I was a tool, which is flattering, because I believe that I'm maybe one of a half-dozen tools that the organization relies on to take care of the issues. But you get to a point when you say, "I'm not a pawn." I knew I had to go because I just wasn't happy. I was miserable and tired of complaining about it.*

By the time Harris came upon the poem, he had already accepted his new job as president and COO of a medical device start-up. A new beginning does not necessarily mean we are finished with the past, and Harris, having promised himself a six-month transition period, was having a terrible time disconnecting from Pharmaco and his mentor, Alfred. The poem he read helped him come to terms with that by simultaneously intensifying his image of what Pharmaco would be like if he stayed and giving him a metaphor for why his leaving was inevitable. His turning point had come three years after he had started trying to find his way to a new career. None of us can snap our fingers to create either unfreezing or jelling events. Is there any way to ensure that we won't miss them altogether?

Preparation Favors Reinvention

"Fortune," said Louis Pasteur, "favors the prepared mind."[12] The story behind his famous dictum illustrates the mechanics of insight in any domain, including career change.

At age fifty-seven, Pasteur was studying chicken cholera. Because of an oversight, he left some batches of bacillus culture, taken from some diseased chickens, unattended in his laboratory over the summer. When he returned in the fall, he injected his chickens with the bacilli out of a relentless spirit of experimentation. To his surprise, the chickens did not die. He concluded that the bacillus cultures had spoiled over the summer and went out to get a new, more potent batch as well as some new chickens. Both old and new chickens were injected with the new culture. The new chickens all died, while the old ones survived. When he realized that all the survivors had been injected once before with the weaker strain, the account tells us that Pasteur "remained silent for a minute, then exclaimed as if he had seen a vision: 'Don't you see they have been vaccinated.' "[13]

Although vaccination against smallpox had already existed for seventy-five years, no one before had hit on the idea of extending vaccination from smallpox to other infectious diseases. Pasteur saw the analogy: His surviving chickens were protected against cholera by the spoiled bacilli just as humans were protected from smallpox by inoculation with cowpox cultures. He also saw a second analogy: The weakening of the cultures left unattended in the lab was akin to the weakening of the smallpox bacilli that happened naturally inside a cow's body. The vaccine for the latter had to be extracted physically from cows. Now Pasteur saw that vaccines could be produced at will in the laboratory.

Discovery literally means uncovering something that has always been there but was hidden from sight by the "blinkers of habit."[14] In the case of vaccination, the blinkers of habit stemmed from the convention that work on vaccination and research on microorganisms took place in separate, previously unconnected fields of scientific practice. Pasteur was ready to make a discovery when a favorable opportunity presented itself because he knew both fields and had primed himself through years of study and hard work.

It is also no accident that the vaccination idea came to Pasteur right after his summer break. Having stepped back from his direct work on cholera, he was able to see his old problem in a new light. This is the famous "incubation" phenomenon, in which, "after ceasing to consciously work on a difficult problem, [artists and scientists] sometimes experience an apparent flash of illumination, during which a solution appears to them unexpectedly."[15] Professional reinvention also requires a stepping back to obtain a new way of seeing what is.[16] The full emotional and cognitive complexity of the change process can only be digested with moments of detachment and time for reflective observation. In the same way, time away from the everyday grind creates the "break frame" that allows people in transition to articulate intellectually what they already knew emotionally.

Stepping Back

The French phrase *reculer pour mieux sauter* literally means "stepping back to better leap forward." It expresses how much we need perspective to arrive at the novel recombination of existing elements that defines an invention or creation.[17] Jane Stevens, a thirty-two-year-old with an M.B.A. in finance, knew something was wrong in her life but could not put her finger on it. Awareness clicked during a solo, ten-hour drive to a college friend's wedding. Five years earlier, while working on her master's degree in international development, Jane had gotten a dream offer, a project with a young firm doing pioneering lending work in Latin America. The project led to a country-manager role, then a position as regional director creating institutions that served the needs of craftspeople known as "microentrepreneurs."

> *I was doing something I really believed in, using a business model that works, and the results were spectacular. But I had stopped feeling fulfilled. Being in consulting was no longer gratifying. And the calculus of my professional and personal lives was changing. I was on the road all the time and wanted to put down some roots. I was not developing my own life and knew I had to invest in myself differently to have a family. And I was working very long hours for nonprofit wages.*

All these things lurked in the back of her mind, but Jane had not had the time or psychological distance to analyze all these elements in tandem. "I was in cognitive dissonance for six months, caught between the growing realization that I wasn't happy and my belief in the vision of my firm." During the ten hours in the car, however, she put together the pieces in a way that led to an obvious conclusion. After that, things happened very quickly. Two weeks later, at her five-year M.B.A. reunion, she reconnected with two former classmates who had acquired a group of firms in the telecommunications industry. By the end of the weekend, they told her they had a new company and they wanted her to run it. A week later, she accepted their formal offer.

Jane was lucky. A relatively short time-out allowed her to break frame; it also enhanced the probability that when something new "drifted by," she would have courage enough to go for it. For others, like Brenda Rayport, the realization that one has been stuck for quite a while in an ill-fitting career provokes a desire for a longer moratorium, a break from active decision making and job hunting. Like so many other people we have seen so far, Brenda only knew what she didn't want to do and that she needed time. When she got married and moved to Chicago, she used the move as an excuse to step back.

The big decision wasn't moving to Chicago. It was deciding not to go back to my firm in a comparable position. I could have done that, and they encouraged me to, but I really didn't want to. I was headhunted by everybody for jobs close to what I had done before. But I didn't want to be part of a company. It was too similar. I didn't see any advantage to it. The problem was, I didn't have a forward trajectory, I couldn't see where I was going. I really wanted a time-out at that point.

I did know that I wanted to be part of a community, so I started getting involved in Jewish activities and arts organizations. This broke me of the need to have an institutional affiliation. I learned how to listen more to myself, to reflect on what I wanted to do and what I enjoyed doing. I included being successful and making money in "enjoy doing," but I had to figure out how to put the pleasure back in to a money-making job.

I thought I wanted to work in education. I volunteered in the public schools. I wanted to see what it's like to teach, to work with eight- and nine-year-olds. An ongoing dialogue with my husband helped me see that wasn't it. He urged me look at what I did back in my twenties, what I fell in love with when I left school. I had loved being an editor. I remember having enormous discussions with him, often pretty anguished ones. I felt editing was women's work. I thought it was a submissive, or subordinate, kind of helping work. I really fought that. I was trying to reposition myself as a kind of market maker.

He would say to me, "Where's the scarcity, Brenda? Is there a scarcity of people who are making deals? Is there a scarcity of people who can put together bulleted lists? No, there's a scarcity of people who can really bring out the best in the people and make great products." That dialogue allowed me to start working as a freelance editor, which was really only a step. I thought it would lead to something else, but I didn't know what. I knew I would be meeting lots of interesting people, that I would be developing a skill again. It was important to me to be able to get in doors and to reestablish a network.

By this time, I had developed a pretty strong point of view about the publishing business. High-quality authors were the scarce commodities. And I thought that being an editor at a publishing house had become a very passive job. It's become totally P&L-oriented, which is neither a creative nor an innovative way to be involved in a business. And with the "disintermediation" that's happening in the business, all of the power was accruing to people other than acquisitions editors—people outside the publishing houses, like agents. Slowly, it began to dawn on me that being an agent might be the absolute best option. I could have more reach than I had ever imagined. I could be true to who I was, and not just by being a deal maker. I mean, there are literary agents who are deal makers, who are very transactional and extremely focused on their relationships with publishers and who do not serve the interests of their authors particularly well. But I knew that that would not be how I would operate. I would stay true to being relational, being concerned about the content of books, being absolutely an authors' agent, because the publishers don't have as much power as they used to have. And I knew this would be a very good selling line to authors.

It is hard for people to achieve the objectivity they need to question and change their daily routines while they are still actively immersed in them. Time-out periods—sometimes as short as Jane's ten-hour drive, other times as long as Brenda's multiyear moratorium—help people make changes by providing a space for reflective observation.[18] Stepping back makes room for insights we have been incubating but cannot yet articulate. It helps us see

the coexistence—and incompatibility—of old and new. Changes
in the habitual rhythm of our work or halts in our normal productive activity can work as triggers, waking us up from our daily
routines and refocusing our attention on change.[19] In a time-out,
attention shifts away from everyday pressures, creating the space
needed to reconsider the future.

Brenda's first reaction to a trigger—the menace of a caricature—was to overcompensate for the void she felt by putting her
career at the bottom of her list of priorities. But stepping back led
her to a more creative solution, in which she combined the best of
all worlds.

*Being an agent gives me a complete career and a complete life.
There's no trade-off. Sure, I get busy and, of course, on any given
task, I have to decide what comes first, my job or my life. My life
is more enjoyable all around. It's not just about work versus personal life. It's about "What's my voice? Can I be creative? Am I
just a corporate drone? Do I just exist as a thank-you in people's
prefaces? Am I a writer?" If someone were to draw that cartoon
of me now, what would I tell the artist about myself? Lots: arts
boards, philanthropy, a dog, a great marriage, a Jewish faith, Pi-
lates, dance class. . . .*

Windows of Opportunity

Julio Gonzales, like many of his fellow students in a one-year
midcareer master's program, approached the end of his sabbatical
with a mix of anxiety and anticipation. That year had given all the
students a chance to design experiments, to make new connections, and to step back from daily routines. A lot had happened in
that year, enough to raise awareness of the problems, but in many
cases, not enough to point to good solutions. Time had run out.
When Julio and his peers started the program, a year had seemed
like an eternity. But major transitions often require two or three
years. Now the questions burning in their minds were: "Can I
take an interim step? If I do that, how do I protect myself from

falling back into the same old, same old? How long do I have before inertia sets in?"

These are very good questions. In a series of studies on the introduction of new technologies (for instance, software engineering tools or graphics software), MIT researchers discovered a *windows of opportunity* effect.[20] They found that managers have only a discrete time period in which to effect a real change after introducing a new technology. After that period, use of the technology tended to "congeal," freezing unresolved problems in the technology and fixing its use in a specific organizational context, at least until the next crisis. Adaptation to new technologies was rarely a smooth, continuous process. Rather, it occurred in fits and stops; whatever changes did not get made at first were put off for much later, usually not until the consequences of those latent problems accumulated to provoke a crisis, opening the next window for change. Research on leaders newly taking charge of organizations shows the same effect: New leaders have a fixed time period in which to make changes; after that, it gets harder.[21]

Nathalie Gaumont, a thirty-nine-year-old French nutritionist and M.B.A., came to understand the windows-of-opportunity effect. In the heat of the moment, she informally accepted an attractive job offer from a former boss. It was the perfect offer, according to Susan Fontaine's logic of CV progression. Nathalie would move up a big notch in prestige and responsibility, moving from heading a European group to overseeing operations worldwide. The new firm, Nomad, was moving up economically, while her current employer was losing market share. But as a senior nutritionist for the European division of a major U.S. food company, she was already feeling burned out; the new job meant even more responsibility, more hours, and more international travel. The one thing she knew was that she wanted less of all that. And the new job offered only an incremental change. Approaching forty, she wondered whether the time was "now or never" to make a sweeping change in her life. But could she pass up a concrete offer that promised at least some change to her professional life?

Reason told her to go for it.

I figured there would be more opportunities for growth—lateral moves, taking on other brands. I can't go any higher at Packard and stay in Europe. And, the company is not doing so well; it's losing market share worldwide. Now I have a staff job and report to a vice president rather than a division head. I'm getting further and further removed from upper management and am losing visibility. I'm spending a lot of time on regulatory issues, lobbying work, when I'd prefer to be closer to the heart of the business. The downside at Nomad is that I'd be reporting to someone based in Japan. The areas Nomad wants to develop are in Latin America and Asia-Pacific. I already travel more than I want to, but at least it's within Europe. At Nomad, I'd have two or three big trips each month. I've tried to ask how much, but the answer is always that it would be up to me. And I just found out the job will not be based in the city, as I thought. That means a long commute each day.

It was confusing. Nathalie had had little time for any activity outside her job, much less time to devote to any kind of concerted job search.

My job has been very intense. I'm very committed and passionate about it. I work every weekend. Two or three times a week I'm on an airplane. I just endure; I'm a good soldier. I let people put stuff on my back. I have a hard time saying no. But I feel that I'm caught in a spiral. Am I going to keep going in circles? Here is change coming to me on a silver platter. It isn't perfect, but it's an escape hatch. I know myself. If I stay here, despite all good intentions, I will easily fall right back into the routine.

Two unexpected events made her question her decision to take the new job. A close friend died, at the age of fifty, from liver cancer. Before she died, she advised Nathalie to get out of the rut and pressure of her business life. Then, a necessary surgical procedure resulted in a one-month medical leave. Nathalie suddenly had time to think through what she really wanted. Jolted by her friend's untimely death, on medical leave she started considering things she never before found time for.

This month, I've had some ideas but they are not precise. I'm interested in doing a thesis on the sociology of eating behaviors, to understand the real barriers to healthy eating. When I was younger, I went to an arts high school and joined a dance company. But then I gave that up when I thought I'd go to medical school. I've been wondering about going back to something in the health field. I think I'd be happy in a medical setting dealing with real people rather than with dossiers and projects. I wonder if I can transfer my business school skills to a health-related NGO like Doctors without Borders.

Realizing that the proposed job change would only delay the serious thinking she needed to do, Nathalie decided to decline the "perfect offer" in order to buy some time to pursue a true career shift. Then, true to her own predictions, she got caught right back in the routine. Two years later, she was still at the first company, still not sure how to move out. Maybe she was not yet ready for change, or maybe one month was not enough time to build momentum. Or maybe failing to start something new in the window right after her leave kept her stuck.

Nathalie's story is a cautionary tale. Windows of opportunity open and close back up again. We go through periods when we are highly receptive to major change and periods when even incremental deviations are hard to tolerate.[22] What we do in the period immediately following a time-out determines whether we will be able to use that experience to effect real change or whether, instead, old routines will reassert themselves, leaving basic problems unresolved until urgency builds the next time around.

Telling Ourselves

At the height of the dot-com craze, at an "Internet boot camp" near Silicon Valley, a thousand people gathered in a ballroom to learn how to become Internet entrepreneurs. PowerPoint presentation after PowerPoint presentation told the audience how to do it. But the real action was between presentations. During the coffee breaks, participants could go to booths, lined up as if going to confession, to tell their stories to and receive feedback from specialists on the "elevator pitch," the two-minute compact story used to talk your way in the door of a new career. The waiting lines were long.

In one of those lines was Roy Holstrom, a fifty-three-year-old mechanical engineer. A victim of his manufacturing firm's last wave of downsizing, Roy had quickly come to the conclusion, in the spirit of Groucho Marx, that he did not want to join any corporation that would have him. He had spent his severance time in the library, searching for patents without a home. After months of research, he had found the needle in a haystack—a solar energy device—and had tracked down the inventor, proposing that they join forces. Now he was at boot camp, hoping to find capital or advisory board members. And to get those, he knew he needed to get the story just right. He was in line for a second round of coaching on his pitch.

People devote considerable energy to developing their stories— what key experiences marked their path; what meanings they attribute to those experiences; and, more importantly, what common thread links old and new.[23] Precisely for that reason, some academics argue that interviewing people about why and how they are changing is a flawed approach. Interviews, the argument goes, just yield a self-presentation: the cleaned-up identity a person puts on for the outside world. They can never unearth the "truth" because, as any good social psychologist will tell us, people can't resist embellishing their stories, making themselves look braver and smarter than they really are and coming up with logical explanations for events that are really random. So our stories never reflect objective reality.

That is why revising our stories is a fundamental tool for reinventing ourselves. One of the central identity problems that has to be worked out during a career transition is deciding on the story that links the old and new self. Until that is solved, the external audience to whom we are selling our reinvention remains dubious, and we too feel unsettled and uncertain of our own identity. To be compelling, the story must explain why we must reinvent ourselves, who we are becoming, and how we will get there. Early versions are always rough drafts. They get floated to friends, families, and new contacts, whose reactions prompt revisions. Since often we don't know exactly where we are going or what the critical events along the way will be, the story will necessarily go through many iterations before it is finalized.

At the very start of a transition, when all we have is a long laundry list of possible selves, it unsettles us that we have no story. We are disturbed to find so many different options appealing, and we worry that the same self who once chose what we no longer want to do, might again make a bad choice. One person in transition out of the finance world put it plainly: "It concerns me that I've opened the array of possibilities so broadly. I want to make sure I'm going in the right direction, that whatever I end up doing is really satisfying. But when I see the different types of opportunities I am considering, I wonder if I know what really is my identity. How do I define myself, and how do others define me?" Julio Gonzales, who had been miserable for years as a heart surgeon, worried about making a change that would threaten his family's financial security. If medicine had been such a misguided choice, how could he know that a different choice would not be equally misguided? To act with assurance—to take a chance on ourselves—we have to make a convincing internal pitch.

Until we have a story, others view us as unfocused. It is harder to get their help. Equally important is having a good story to tell others, putting it into the public sphere even before it is fully formed. By making public declarations about what we seek and what common thread binds our old and new selves, we clarify our intentions and improve our ability to enlist others' support. Like Roy Holstrom's elevator pitch, this is partially a problem of self-marketing. We need someone to take a chance on us since, by definition, we are moving into a new and unproven realm. Potential employers or coworkers come to know (and therefore, trust) us when they know our story and can accept it as legitimate. Sometimes it takes many rehearsals before it comes out just right. What happens in the retelling is not just a more polished story; we finally settle on a narrative that can inform the next step.

When stuck in the morass of the transition period, we hope desperately for a defining moment that will impel us to quick and decisive action. We wait for an epiphany when the clouds part and everything clarifies. But the causal sequence is really the other way around: Insight is an effect, not a cause; our diffuse hopes and dissatisfactions jell when we are getting close, the result of having struggled and floundered in the transition. There is not much we can do to manufacture the turning points that lend dramatic form to our stories. But when events happen that serve our purposes, we can weave them into the fabric of our reinvention narratives to use them to explain—to ourselves as much as to others—why we are changing.

part 3

putting the unconventional strategies to work

eight

becoming yourself

I F WE KNEW from the start what it meant to be fully ourselves, finding a new career would be so much easier. But because we are growing and changing all the time, the oft-cited key to a better working life, "knowing yourself," turns out to be the prize at the end of the journey rather than the light at its beginning. Whether we feel closer to Pierre Gerard, who as a teenager felt a calling to minister to the suffering, or to Lucy Hartman, who stumbled through twenty years of technical and managerial jobs before finding her mission as a professional coach, there is no substitute for constant exploration. We don't find ourselves in a blinding flash of insight, and neither do we change overnight. We learn by doing, and each new experience is part answer and part question.

The stories we have read illustrate that identity transitions unfold as cycles of changes (as summarized in figure 8-1) in which our early images of possible selves lead to the limbolike state when we live and work between provisional identities; with several loops around this cycle, we eventually undergo a more profound change that allows fuller expression of whom we have become.

Progress in this cycle only comes with practice. Experiments, connections, and the sense we make of them are the tangible "hooks" we use to test our possible selves, making them more real, more "implementable." The cumulative effects of putting identity in practice change what we do, how we work, and what work means in the broader context of our lives.

FIGURE 8 - 1

Working Identity

SUMMARY OF THE TRANSITION PROCESS AND PRACTICES THAT PROMOTE SUCCESSFUL CHANGE

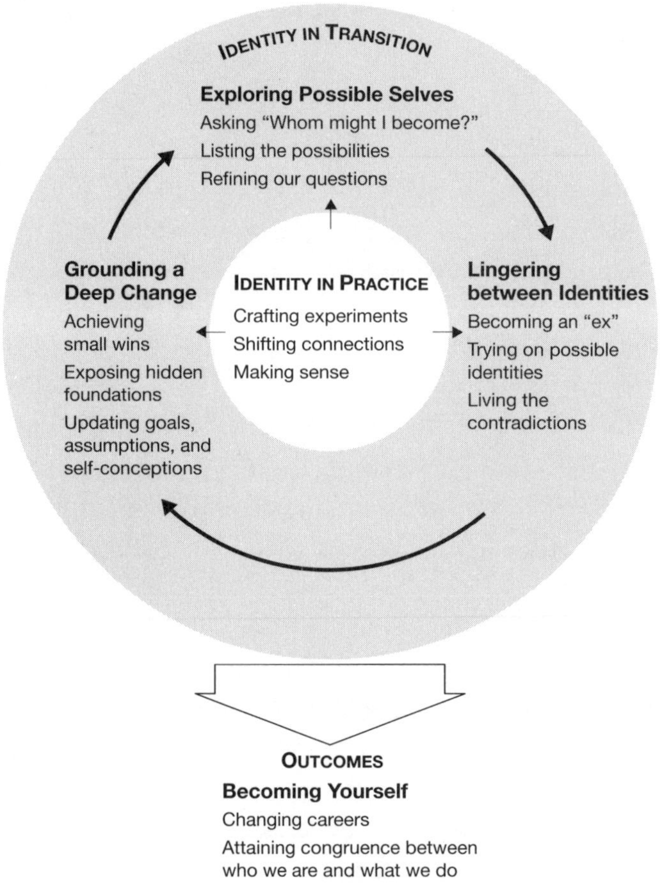

IDENTITY IN TRANSITION

Exploring Possible Selves
Asking "Whom might I become?"
Listing the possibilities
Refining our questions

Grounding a Deep Change
Achieving small wins
Exposing hidden foundations
Updating goals, assumptions, and self-conceptions

IDENTITY IN PRACTICE
Crafting experiments
Shifting connections
Making sense

Lingering between Identities
Becoming an "ex"
Trying on possible identities
Living the contradictions

OUTCOMES
Becoming Yourself
Changing careers
Attaining congruence between who we are and what we do

Change takes time because we usually have to cycle through identifying and testing possibilities a few times, asking better questions with each round of tests, crafting better experiments, and building on what we have learned before. Two different rhythms regulate this cycle. Speed is of the essence in moving from making a list of possible selves—in our heads or on paper—to actually testing any one of them. If it seems that relatively few people make the career changes they dream about it is because many of us just don't take the first step. Which self we test hardly matters; small steps like embarking on a new project or going to a night course can ignite a process that changes everything. But, paradoxically, it is usually better to slow down in the testing phase, investing enough time to explore even those selves that seem less promising. We need time to fully internalize the self-knowledge we are accumulating with each experience. Even when taking our time seems unproductive, it is hardly so; we are moving away from outdated images of what we "ought" to be, of meeting expectations or pleasing others—the hidden foundation that dictated our old working identity—and moving toward greater self-direction.[1]

The reinvention process challenges us to redefine ourselves. But, contrary to popular belief, working our identities is not an exercise in abstraction or introspection; it is a messy trial-and-error process of *learning by doing* in which experience in the here and now (not in the distant past) helps to evolve our ideas about what is plausible—and desirable. The most typical problem at midcareer is not defining what kind of work we find enjoyable and meaningful. Rather, it is figuring out how to transfer old preferences and values to new and different contexts and how to integrate those with changing priorities and newly blooming potential. It is a problem of recombining and reanchoring. And the "solution" is never the job change itself. Self-creation is a lifelong journey. Only by our actions do we learn who we want to become, how best to travel, and what else will need to change to ease the way.

Variations on the Theme

Throughout this book, we have looked for commonalities in the process and practice of working identity. Before we extract some general guidelines about getting started, a few words are in order about how different groups of people might experience career reinvention differently. Although the most important lessons lie in the similarities across stories rather than in isolated differences, benchmarking our own experience with those people most like ourselves—in occupation, life circumstances, or degree of direction for change—is a useful exercise.

All reinvention stories do not start alike. Some people quit their jobs to make space before they have figured out what they want to do next; others stay, if only nominally, in old roles until the leap is a forgone conclusion. Which of these two paths we take is partially determined by the nature of our old career.

Generally, professionals—consultants, lawyers, financial services professionals, academics, and, to a lesser degree, physicians—are much more likely to continue in their jobs until the new identity is close to fully formed, or at least to withhold quitting until a possible avenue is fairly well defined. Professionals also seem to have an easier time finding ideas for a new career. The reasons have little to do with graduate-education credentials and much to do with the nature of professional work. Professionals simply have more autonomy over their work schedules than do most other occupational groups. They can come into the office late or leave early and take days off when they need them (of course, the quid pro quo includes long hours, missed vacations, and taking work home over weekends). Professionals always have at least one foot on the outside—in their work with clients and their frequent interaction with members of the same profession in the world at large—and that always helps when it comes to reinvention.

Managers bogged down by all manner of internal meetings typically do not have a fraction of that freedom or flexibility. Consequently, they are more likely to suffer from tunnel vision, more likely to need to stop, rest up, and refuel before starting to think about something new. Executive education courses play such a catalytic role for managers precisely because they get them out of the office. That tunnel vision, however, is also the reason why executive programs often involve enough time away to awaken a desire for change but rarely last long enough to point to a new direction. Finding additional ways of stepping back is especially critical for this population; negotiating sabbaticals, chunking up vacations, moving to freelance work, or simply chucking it all without a safety net, are frequently used tactics by managers wanting to move on to the next thing.[2]

The less time we've had to craft experiments, shift our professional connections, and make sense of it all, the more we may need a longer time-out; creative solutions take time and space to surface. Some people, like Gary McCarthy, end up taking more than one sabbatical—one to recharge batteries, another to focus on finding the new career. People who have lost their jobs (even if they have taken a voluntary severance package) are at the greatest risk of short-circuiting the process, since they don't have the option of staggering their time-outs. Carving a smaller time-out within a longer fallow period—declaring a three-month moratorium on talking to headhunters or working the job sites, during which we give ourselves permission to explore things we enjoy doing even though they are unlikely leads to a next career—can make all the difference in the mind-set we bring to the transition process.[3]

One major premise of this book is that we must reverse the conventional "thinking before doing" logic to successfully change careers. That is not easy to do or to explain in our goal-driven society. Taking a sabbatical or going back to school is a socially accepted, "legitimate" way to dedicate ourselves to exploration, to following crooked paths. Freed from the everyday working world, detours and serendipity not only become possible; they become our purpose. A sabbatical temporarily suspends the rules and demarcates a protected milieu in which we can toy with possibilities, knowing we will return to reality again soon. In the interim, we can test unformed, even risky or conflicting, identities in a secure environment, incubating provisional identities until we are ready to claim one or more as truly our selves.

Women tend to make more use of time-outs as reinvention strategies than men, for simple social and economic reasons. Across cultures and occupation groups, it is still more acceptable for a woman to say that she is taking time to "find herself" than it is for a man. It is also more likely to be economically feasible: Within the college-educated population that is the subject of this book, women are more likely than men to have partners whose incomes are sufficient to maintain a basic lifestyle. Moreover, in highly educated, relatively affluent circles, men are still more likely to be the primary breadwinners. But that is changing, and I encountered several instances in which members of a couple took turns at reinvention.

Obviously, the larger context matters, too. Societal cycles of economic prosperity and social change can affect the timing and form of professional renewal. The study at the heart of this book, however, spanned from the Internet heyday of the late 1990s to the gloomier turn of the millennium; it showed that the process of renewal unfolds similarly even in leaner economic times.

Another dimension on which to compare and contrast experiences concerns the outcomes of the career changes. Throughout the study, one question came up more frequently than any other: Did anyone regret the move into the new? Many people said they made at least one "wrong" move. But they learned from their mistakes and moved on to something else, adjusting their course based on their experiences. Of course, there is always an element of rationalization: After the fact, we easily conclude that we did the best we could. People did make trade-offs: Some struggled with lower incomes when they chose to pursue their passion, and others gave up some measure of challenge or intellectual stimulation in pursuit of a more secure future. But I heard great regret only from those who failed to act, who were unable or unwilling to put their dreams to the test and to find out for themselves if there were better alternatives. The only wrong move consisted of no move.

So can anyone, regardless of education, social class, or gender, make a major change at midcareer? The combined experiences of Pierre and Lucy, Gary and Dan, Susan, Brenda and all the others suggest that the answer is yes. The real question is, "Under what conditions are people able to break with the past and plunge into a new and happier future?"

Unconventional Strategies

This book started by warning the reader that there was no tenpoint plan for making a career change. But some important general guidelines emerge from the many stories told here. This section distills those guidelines as a set of nine unconventional strategies for reinventing your career: act, then reflect; flirt with your selves; live the contradictions; make big change in small steps; experiment with new roles; find people who are what you want to be; don't wait for a catalyst; step back periodically but not for too long; and seize windows of opportunity.

- **Unconventional strategy 1:** *Act your way into a new way of thinking and being. You cannot discover yourself by introspection.*

  Start by changing what you do. Try different paths. Take action, and then use the feedback from your actions to figure out what you think, feel, and want. Don't try to analyze or plan your way into a new career. Conventional strategies advocated by self-assessment manuals and traditional career counselors would have you start by looking inside. Start instead by stepping out. Be attentive to what each step teaches you, and make sure that each step helps you take the next.

- **Unconventional strategy 2:** *Stop trying to find your one true self. Focus your attention on which of your many possible selves you want to test and learn more about.*

Reflection is important. But we can use it as a defense against testing reality; reflecting on who we are is less important than probing whether we really want what we think we want. Acting in the world gives us the opportunity to see our selves through our behaviors and allows us to adjust our expectations as we learn. In failing to act, we hide from ourselves.

- **Unconventional strategy 3:** *Allow yourself a transition period in which it is okay to oscillate between holding on and letting go. Better to live the contradictions than to come to a premature resolution.*

  The years preceding a career change necessarily involve difficulty, turmoil, confusion, and uncertainty.[4] One of the hardest tasks of reinvention is staying the course when it feels like you are coming undone. Unfortunately, there is no alternative but foreclosure—retreating from change either by staying put or taking the wrong next job. Watch out for decisions made in haste, especially when it comes to unsolicited offers. It takes a while to move from old to new. Those who try to short-circuit the process often just end up taking longer.

- **Unconventional strategy 4:** *Resist the temptation to start by making a big decision that will change everything in one fell swoop. Use a strategy of* small wins, *in which incremental gains lead you to more profound changes in the basic assumptions that define your work and life. Accept the crooked path.*

  Small steps lead to big changes, so don't waste time, energy, and money on finding the "answer" or the "lever" that, when pushed, will have dramatic effects. Almost no one gets change right on the first try. Forget about moving in a straight line. You will probably have to cycle through a few times, letting what you learn inform the next cycle. You will know that you are learning at a deeper level when you start to question what aspects of your life apart from your job also need changing.

- **Unconventional strategy 5:** *Identify projects that can help you get a feel for a new line of work or style of working. Try to do these as extracurricular activities or parallel paths so that you can experiment seriously without making a commitment.*

  Think in terms of side projects and temporary assignments, not binding decisions. Pursue these activities seriously, but delay commitment. Slowly ascertain your enduring values and preferences, what makes you unique in the world. Just make sure that you vary your experiments, so that you can compare and contrast experiences before you narrow your options.

- **Unconventional strategy 6:** *Don't just focus on the work. Find people who are what you want to be and who can provide support for the transition. But don't expect to find them in your same old social circles.*

  Break out of your established network. Branch out. Look for role models—people who give you glimpses of what you might become and who are living examples of different ways of working and living. Most of us seek to change not only what we do; we also aspire to work with people we like and respect and with whom we enjoy spending our precious time.

- **Unconventional strategy 7:** *Don't wait for a cataclysmic moment when the truth is revealed. Use everyday occurrences to find meaning in the changes you are going through. Practice telling and retelling your story. Over time, it will clarify.*

  Major career transitions take three to five years. The big "turning point," if there is one, tends to come late in the story. In the interim, make use of anything as a trigger. Don't wait for a catalyst. What you make of events is more important than the events themselves. Take advantage of whatever life sends your way to revise, or at least reconsider, your story. Practice telling it in different ways to different people, in much the same way you would revise a résumé and cover letter for different jobs. But don't just tell the story to a friendly audience; try it out on skeptics. And don't be disturbed when the story changes along the way.

- **Unconventional strategy 8:** *Step back. But not for too long.*
  When you get stuck and are short on insight, take time to step back from the fray to reflect on how and why you are changing. Even as short a break as a day's hike in the country can remove the blinders of habit. But don't stay gone too long, or it will be hard to reel yourself back in. Only through interaction and active engagement in the real world do we discover ourselves.

- **Unconventional strategy 9:** *Change happens in bursts and starts. There are times when you are open to big change and times when you are not. Seize opportunities.*
  Windows of opportunity open and close back up again. We go through periods when we are highly receptive to major change and periods when even incremental deviations from "the plan" are hard to tolerate.[5] Take advantage of any natural windows (e.g., the period just after an educational program or assuming a new position; a milestone birthday) to start off on the right foot. Communicate to others that you have changed (and will be making more changes). Watch out for the insidious effect of old routines. Progress can be served by hanging in limbo, asking questions, allowing time and space to linger between identities. But don't let unanswered questions bog you down; move on, even if to an interim commitment.

Identity, Lost and Regained

Psychologist Erik Erikson once wrote that identity is like a good conscience: It is never maintained once and for all but constantly lost and regained. Adult development, he argued, is a process that requires both questioning and commitment.[6] The person who neither questions nor commits to a course of action obviously goes nowhere. Questioning that does not lead to a new (or renewed) commitment, as in the case of the perpetual student or the devoted dilettante, is not much better. Commitment without questioning produces an "organization man" who has no identity beyond title and function. To be a growing adult means to make commitments that are informed by prior questioning. As one of the career changers in this study put it, "There are two types of people. Some are always jumping. Some never jump—they settle down too easily and get stuck."

Self-renewal requires some jumping and some settling back in. The kind of reinvention considered here is not a personality makeover; it is a process and practice that allows us to get back in touch with forgotten selves, to reorder priorities, and to explore long-standing or newfound interests. As in most voyages of discovery, the end points are never quite as we imagined them, and they are rarely the ones we originally charted. Sometimes all we know at the start is that we want to be somewhere else. "The end of all our exploring," as T. S. Eliot reminds us, "will be to arrive where we started and know the place for the first time." In between, we try on unfamiliar roles and experiment with trial identities, always updating our goals and methods, with each step coming closer and closer to becoming ourselves again.

studying career transitions

H OW DO PEOPLE CHANGE CAREERS? Organizational researchers have rarely asked this question so simply and
straightforwardly. Certainly, many have studied how people adapt
to new work roles and how their organizations teach them the
ropes by putting them through formal and informal socialization
experiences. But most of this research was done in the time of the
"one career" career.[1] We learned a lot about what accounts for ad-
vancement and mobility within a single path but created relatively
little knowledge of the sort that might be useful to the person who
seeks a change of path.[2]

Whereas career reinvention is by no means a new phenomenon—we can look to Dante Alighieri, who wrote the *Divine
Comedy* at forty, and Paul Gauguin, who quit his career as a stockbroker and fled to Tahiti to become a painter—the demise of life-
time employment has made the topic more pressing. The "new
career," as defined by researchers Michael Arthur and Douglas Hall,

among others, is a boundaryless and protean sequence of experiences summarized by the following trends:[3]

- **Mobility:** Greater frequency of career moves across employers and careers

- **Reputations built from the outside in:** Validation and marketability derived more and more from peoples' reputation outside their employer firm

- **Create-your-own career paths:** Disappearance of external guides for sequences of work experiences and traditional corporate career planning; emergence of internal, self-generated guides; rise of portfolio and project careers

- **Pursuit of meaning:** Enterprise viewed as a path to the expression of deeply held identities and values

- **Balance and flexibility:** Boundaries between work and nonwork life blur; personal and family reasons play more important roles than before in choices and decisions

Despite the trends, the study of career transitioning is still in its infancy. There is plenty of how-to advice, but we still know precious little about exactly how people change careers. "How" one changes careers is a very different question from "when" or "with what frequency within a given population." It is also a different question from "What antecedent factors—for example, personality, IQ, risk profile, or quality of network—make the process go faster or more smoothly?" This book breaks new ground by simply focusing on the "how" question and its corollary, "What conditions enable or inhibit taking the leap?" These questions and aims guided the selection of case studies on which the book is based.

Theoretical Background

The study and the model of the reinvention process that emerged from it were guided by the simple idea that changing careers amounts to changing identities. My aim was to investigate how changes in one coincide with or provoke changes in the other and to understand the dual nature of reinvention: the change that happens inside, in one's private self-conceptions, and the change that unfolds outside, in the real and public world of concrete possibilities and choices. I informed these working hypotheses with theories of learning-by-doing and theories about identity-as-possibility.[4]

Explaining how and why people change as they navigate career transitions necessarily raises fundamental questions about what exactly changes—and can change—at midcareer. My starting assumption, based on the work of MIT psychologist and career development expert Edgar Schein, was that the changes that occur during a career transition are changes in the nature and integration of a person's social selves and not in basic personality structure or patterns of psychological defenses.[5] But research also indicates that the identity changes that follow a period of major questioning and exploration are not limited only to competencies, attitudes, and behavior; they may also entail a rather drastic reorganization of the basic priorities and organizing principles that structure a person's life.[6]

Studying career transitions also raises fundamental questions about how change unfolds: What are the change mechanisms? What is the sequence of events? Here I turned to theories about evolutionary change and adaptation to conceptualize reinvention as unfolding through iterative learning cycles in which we generate a variety of possible selves, select some for closer exploration, and eventually retain some and discard others.[7] My interest in what happens during the period in between the old and new career next led me to theories about transitions, boundaries, and rites of passage in psychoanalysis and anthropology. I combined ideas from these varied perspectives to understand what occurs during the critical in-between period.

Selecting the Case Studies

The study evolved from the follow-up to an earlier project, in which I investigated how young professionals advanced (or failed to advance) within their firms' up-or-out hierarchies. The transition entailed moving from junior, technical, and managerial roles to senior, client-advisory, and revenue-generating positions. Doing an informal follow-up several years after the study was completed, I stumbled onto an interesting natural experiment: Among my study group, some had taken the leap to new and different careers, others were actively planning their escape routes (of these, some with greater promise and optimism than others), and still others were happily continuing onward and upward.

The time was 1999 and the Internet craze was raging. I decided to interview new and would-be Web entrepreneurs, as a point of contrast to the consultants and bankers trying to make their way out of their golden handcuffs. That first subgroup eventually expanded to include a range of people moving from large established firms to start-ups. A *Newsweek* cover headline captured the ethos of the times: "Everyone's getting rich but me."[8] As another point of contrast, I decided to find a comparison group of people motivated to change careers by a very different set of drivers: social contribution. That led to a series of interviews with people moving from the private to the nonprofit sector.

Another, somewhat overlapping, subset of career changers grew out of my interest in professional careers —in consulting, investment banking, law, and health care. While teaching senior executives from those groups how to retain their best and brightest, I grew more and more interested in what was driving midcareer professionals out and how they prepared their exits. To vary what had started as a predominantly M.B.A. and business background sample, I looked for lawyers, physicians, university professors, and IT professionals who embarked on career transitions that entailed changing occupations.

My case selection process by no means followed a logic of random sampling. Instead, I relied on what qualitative researchers Barney Glaser and Anslem Strauss call "theoretical sampling" and the "constant comparative method." I added new cases all along, comparing and contrasting the ones I had already to determine whether there were gaps in my coverage of types of transition and selecting new categories and cases to fill those gaps.

The people in my final sample exemplify many varieties and degrees of career reinvention. Some made significant changes in the *context* in which they work, most typically jumping from large, established companies to small, entrepreneurial organizations or to self-employment. Others made major changes in the *content* of the work itself, sometimes leaving an occupation, such as medicine or law, for which they had trained many years. Most made significant changes in both context and content, but most important, they experienced a *subjective feeling of reaching a crossroad,* one that would require psychological change. I settled on a definition of career change that encompassed these three elements.

The sample is certainly biased in that it consists of people who had already started the transition or taken the leap; therefore, it was a group prone to nonconservative response. I do not consider that this poses any challenge to the validity of my arguments, however, because my aim is not to predict who will or will not change careers. Rather, it is to identify the basic tasks of reinvention.

Study Demographics

The people interviewed for this study ranged in age from thirty-two to fifty-one, with most between thirty-eight and forty-three, squarely at midcareer.[9] The reason I chose this age range was not to coincide with the famous "midlife crisis" but rather to study a group of people with enough experience to both know themselves and to make changing careers a high-stakes endeavor. Professional identity, Edgar Schein argues, develops over time with varied experiences and meaningful feedback that allow people to discover their central and enduring preferences, talents, and values, which he termed their "career anchors."[10] Following his definition, my objective was to study people with enough experience to have already developed a sense of working identity in the old career. The people in my sample had invested at least eight to ten years in their previous career paths—and many had invested more—when they began to question the fit of those careers with either enduring or new preferences.

Sixty-five percent of the participants are men; 35 percent are women; 74 percent were married at the start of their transition. Since I conducted part of the study while on a sabbatical from Harvard in France, I added French and British subsamples to the U.S. group in order to diversify in terms of national background and country of residency. Almost half (46 percent) live and work outside the United States. It is a highly credentialed sample: All have college degrees, and about 74 percent have graduate degrees (e.g., business, science, law, and so on).

Interview Method

For the core study, I conducted thirty-nine in-depth interviews. The group included people at different stages of transition. Some were in the midst of making the career change or starting to contemplate a change; others had taken the leap already. Some of the interviews, therefore, were retrospective. In many cases, however, I followed a person over a period of several years, from an early desire to make a change through the in-between period to the actual leap to a new career (and, in a few cases, as he or she circled back to a second search after moving into something that did not work out for the long term).

To track the trajectories of the ongoing process subsample, I conducted an average of three interviews with each person over a period of two years. The initial interview was open-ended, often beginning with the question "Tell me about your career to date" (see figure A-1 for a typical interview protocol). Between the interviews, I had informal e-mail exchanges and telephone conversations with participants to keep track of their progress. Many of them regularly sent me updates.

I conducted all the interviews between July 1999 and December 2001. Interviews typically lasted two hours, ranging from one to three hours. Most of the interviews were tape-recorded and transcribed verbatim. In some cases, when a person was more at ease without the tape recorder, I took extensive handwritten notes,

FIGURE A - 1

Interview Guide

Retrospective interview

- Tell me about your career to date.
- Why did you change careers?
- How long did it take?
- Tell me about the transition period.
- Who made a difference? Why?
- How many different kinds of ideas or possibilities did you consider? How far did you go with each?
- What was the hardest thing about the whole process?
- Apart from the change of job, did you make other changes in your work and life?

Change-in-progress interview

- Why do you want to (or why did you) leave X?
- What ideas do (did) you have about alternatives?
- Which ones are you actively exploring (did you actively explore) and how?
- Who has been helpful or inspiring for you and your thought process? Who hasn't been helpful?
- How would you describe this transition period? What has been the hardest?
- Have you come to any conclusions or eliminated any options?

which I transcribed at the earliest possible time after the interview, never more than two days later.

I supplemented the core study with many shorter interviews with other people in transition as well as with a range of career-change professionals, including headhunters, venture capitalists, career counselors, and outplacement specialists. I also attended a host of career-change seminars, events, and conferences. To provide further context and to verify my findings, I polled my executive education students in the United States and Europe about their career paths and ambitions and honed my ideas by using them in the classroom as teaching material for classes on career development. I conducted public workshops on career reinvention in which I gathered many more stories and points of view. I searched for articles from the business and popular press, for existing case studies or reinvention memoirs from a wider set of people in transition in order to refine my thinking about the applicability of these ideas across a range of career moves.

Analyzing the Interviews

The research design is a multiple-case study in which the cases are treated as a series of independent experiments that confirm or disconfirm conceptual insights. Since my objective was to generate rather than to test theory, I designed the study in an open-ended fashion to allow unplanned themes to emerge from the data.

The analysis of the interviews followed an inductive grounded theory development process.[11] In the early stages of interviewing and analyzing interview transcripts, I searched the data for categories that reflected similarities across participants on types of career-change trajectories. Three rough categories of career-change strategies emerged almost immediately: 1) growing a side project; 2) generating job offers or temporary assignments by talking to headhunters and canvassing old friends and coworkers; and 3) taking a sabbatical or time-out from full-time work, usually to go back to school or take courses. As these categories emerged, I used the theoretical sampling approach to make sure I had enough examples of each type to afford comparison.

In the next stage of the data collection and analysis, I used an iterative process of moving back and forth between the data; the relevant literature in psychology, sociology, and organizational behavior; and my emerging concepts to begin to develop more abstract conceptual categories. Following the methods described by Robert Sutton and Kathleen Eisenhardt, I compared my emerging conceptual model; data from the study; and the literature on identity, career adaptation, and professional socialization to guide decisions about what other kinds of people to interview and what other themes to develop.[12] Along the way, new case studies raised fresh questions; new rounds of comparing and contrasting the case studies sharpened and differentiated the contours of the conceptual categories. As new concepts or categories emerged, either from the literature or the data, I searched the other to find evidence for the theme or to refine it conceptually.

The result is a conception of working identity as both noun and verb: a set of self-conceptions in transition that people work and rework like "working drafts" for whom they might become. In practice, they elaborate, revise, and update these possibilities, allowing them to grow in contour and detail until a fully grounded new working identity emerges.

notes

one

1. Richard T. Pascale, Linda Gioja, and Mark Millemann, *Surfing the Edge of Chaos* (New York: Crown Business, 2000), 14.

2. The name Pierre Gerard is a pseudonym. In order to assure anonymity, I used pseudonyms for all participants in my research study. In addition, particular details of their lives, such as where they live or where they worked before the career change, have been altered.

3. Hazel Markus and Paula Nurius, "Possible Selves," *American Psychologist* 41, no. 9 (1986): 954–969.

4. William Bridges, *Transitions: Making Sense of Life's Changes* (Cambridge, MA: Perseus, 1980).

two

1. Richard Nelson Bolles, *What Color Is Your Parachute?: A Practical Manual for Job-Hunters and Career-Changers,* 31st ed. (Berkeley, CA: Ten Speed Press, 2000).

2. Perri Capell, "Taking the Painless Path to a New Career," *Wall Street Journal Europe,* 2 January 2002.

3. This dichotomy is based on Gilbert Ryle's famous discussion of the difference between "knowing that" and "knowing how." See Ryle, *The Concept of Mind* (Chicago: University of Chicago Press, 1949).

4. Edgar H. Schein, *Career Anchors: Discovering Your Real Values,* rev. ed. (San Diego, CA: University Associates, 1990).

5. Donald A. Schön, *The Reflective Practitioner: How Professionals Think in Action* (New York: Basic Books, 1983).

6. Ikujiro Nonaka, "A Dynamic Theory of Organizational Knowledge Creation," *Organization Science 5*, no. 1 (1994): 14–37.

7. Edgar H. Schein has talked about this as the distinction between "planned change" and "managed learning" in "Kurt Lewin's Change Theory in the Field and in the Classroom: Notes Toward a Model of Managed Learning," *Systems Practice 9*, no. 1 (1996): 27–48.

8. Henry Mintzberg, "Crafting Strategy," *Harvard Business Review 65*, no. 4 (1987): 66–75.

9. See Richard L. Daft and Karl E. Weick, "Toward a Model of Organizations as Interpretation Systems," *Academy of Management Review 9*, no. 2 (1984): 284–295, for a discussion of the distinction between discovering and creating possibilities.

10. Schein, "Kurt Lewin's Change Theory in the Field and in the Classroom," 27–48.

11. Daniel J. Levinson, *The Season's of a Man's Life* (New York: Knopf, 1985).

12. Robert Kegan, *The Evolving Self: Problem and Process in Human Development* (Cambridge, MA: Harvard University Press, 1982).

13. See, for example, Paul D. Tieger, Barbara Barron-Tieger, and Deborah Baker, *Do What You Are: Discover the Perfect Career for You Through the Secrets of Personality Type*, 3d ed. (Boston: Little, Brown, 2001).

14. Anselm L. Strauss, *Mirrors and Masks: The Search for Identity* (London: Martin Robertson, 1977), 91.

15. Hazel Markus and Paula Nurius, "Possible Selves," *American Psychologist 41*, no. 9 (1986): 954–969.

three

1. See William Bridges, *Transitions: Making Sense of Life's Changes* (Cambridge, MA: Perseus, 1980) and Roger L. Gould, *Transformations: Growth and Change in Adult Life* (New York: Simon & Schuster, 1978).

2. Daniel J. Levinson, *The Seasons of a Woman's Life* (New York: Random House, 1997), 29.

3. Samuel D. Osherson, *Holding On and Letting Go: Men and Career Change at Midlife* (New York: Free Press, 1980).

4. Helen Rose Fuchs Ebaugh, *Becoming an Ex: The Process of Role Exit* (Chicago: University of Chicago Press, 1988), 143.

5. Diane Vaughan, *Uncoupling—Turning Points in Intimate Relationships* (New York: Vintage Books, 1990).

6. Ebaugh, *Becoming an Ex*, 110–111.

7. Bridges, *Transitions*, 96–102.

8. Harriet Rubin, *Soloing: Realizing Your Life's Ambition*, 1st ed. (New York: HarperInformation, 1999), 31.

9. Bridges, *Transitions*, 114.

10. See Herminia Ibarra, "Provisional Selves: Experimenting with Image and Identity in Professional Adaptation," *Administrative Science Quarterly* 44, no. 4 (December 1999): 764–791, and John H. Yost, Michael J. Strube, and James R. Bailey, "The Construction of the Self: An Evolutionary View," *Current Psychology* 11, no. 2 (1992): 110–121.

11. Osherson, *Holding on and Letting Go*.

four

1. The idea that change results from bold strokes or long marches is borrowed from Rosabeth M. Kanter, Barry A. Stein, and Todd D. Jick, *The Challenge of Organizational Change: How Companies Experience It and Leaders Guide It* (New York: Free Press, 1992).

2. Karl E. Weick, "Small Wins: Redefining the Scale of Social Problems," *American Psychologist* 39, no. 1 (January 1984): 40–49.

3. Elizabeth P. McKenna, *When Work Does Not Work Anymore: Women, Work, and Identity* (New York, Dell, 1998), 161–162.

4. Adapted from Edgar H. Schein, *Organizational Culture and Leadership*, 2d ed. (San Francisco: Jossey-Bass, 1992), 17.

5. Edgar H. Schein, *Career Anchors: Discovering Your Real Values*, rev. ed. (San Diego, CA: University Associates, 1990). The original anchors identified by Schein are technical or functional competence, general managerial competence, autonomy/independence, security/stability, entrepreneurial creativity, and pure challenge. Later studies reveal two additional anchors: lifestyle and service/dedication to a cause.

Once developed through varied experience, Schein finds that anchors do not change much. A person might experiment with different kinds of work or sacrifice temporarily what they love most in order to meet other goals, but fundamentally, once anchors have formed, people tend to rely on them when and if they can, and most career changers wind their way back to settings and activities that allow them to stay tethered to the things they care most deeply about. Basic assumptions, however, operate at a deeper level, and define whether we are able to keep our anchors while stripping them of the detritus that can muck up the line.

6. The idea of exposing basic assumptions is similar to the notion of "double-loop" learning. Chris Argyris and Donald A. Schön, *Organizational*

Learning: A Theory of Action Perspective (Reading, MA: Addison-Wesley, 1978).

7. Robert Kegan, *The Evolving Self: Problem and Process in Human Development* (Boston: Harvard University Press, 1982). Kegan argues that adults develop in stages, moving out of an "interpersonal" system of making sense, in which others' expectations drive our choices, to an "institutional" system, in which we overidentify with organizations and make decisions that might conflict with personal priorities out of an exaggerated sense of duty. In his theory the final, most mature stage is the "interdependent" system, in which people and institutions are important to our identity but no longer all-encompassing determinants of it.

five

1. Donald A. Schön, *The Reflective Practitioner: How Professionals Think in Action* (New York: Basic Books, 1983).

2. Adapted from Karl E. Weick, *The Social Psychology of Organizing,* 2d ed. (New York: McGraw-Hill, 1979).

3. Karl E. Weick cites this as one of the key advantages of the small-wins strategy. See "Small Wins: Redefining the Scale of Social Problems," *American Psychologist* 39, no. 1 (January 1984): 40–49.

4. Ibid., 43.

5. Hope Dlugozima, James Scott, and David Sharp, *Six Months Off: How to Plan, Negotiate, and Take the Break You Need without Burning Bridges or Going Broke* (New York: Henry Holt, 1996); Joshua White and Susan Griffith, *Taking a Career Break* (Oxford, UK: Vacation Work Publications, 2001).

6. James G. March, "The Technology of Foolishness," in *Ambiguity and Choice in Organizations,* ed. James G. March and Johan Olsen (Bergen: Universitetsforlaget, 1972).

7. Max H. Bazerman, Ann E. Tenbrunsel, and Kimberly Wade-Benzoni, "Negotiating with Yourself and Losing: Making Decisions with Competing Internal Preferences," *Academy of Management Review* 23, no. 2 (April 1998): 225–241.

8. Ibid.

9. Antonio R. Damasio, *Descartes' Error: Emotion, Reason and the Human Brain* (New York: Avon, 1995).

10. Adam Phillips, *On Flirtation* (Cambridge, MA: Harvard University Press, 1994), xvii.

11. Barry M. Staw, Lance E. Sandelands, and Jane E. Dutton, "Threat Rigidity Effects in Organizational Behavior: A Multilevel Analysis," *Administrative Science Quarterly* 26, no. 4 (1981): 501–524.

six

1. Robert J. Lifton, *The Protean Self: Human Resilience in an Age of Fragmentation* (Chicago: University of Chicago Press, 1993), 120.

2. Mark S. Granovetter, "The Strength of Weak Ties," *American Journal of Sociology* 78, no. 6 (1973): 1360–1380; and *Getting a Job: A Study in Contacts and Careers,* 2d ed. (Chicago: University of Chicago Press, 1995). Many of the "weak ties" activated by Granovetter's job hunters were connections developed earlier in their careers that had been dormant.

3. A relatively large fraction of job changes are made without a highly active search, and often without any explicit search at all, via informal networks. Apart from personal referrals, the two other most successful job change methods are applying via a headhunter and building on previous experience as an independent contractor for the firm. See Peter V. Marsden and Elizabeth H. Gorman, "Social Networks, Job Changes, and Recruitment," in *Sourcebook on Labor Markets: Evolving Structures and Processes,* eds. Ivar E. Berg and Arne L. Kalleberg (New York: Kluwer Academic/Plenum Publishers, 2001), 467–502.

4. Roy F. Baumeister, *Identity: Cultural Change and the Struggle for Self* (New York: Oxford University Press, 1986).

5. For a thorough review of research on how relationships help to buffer or change self-conceptions, see Roy F. Baumeister, "The Self," in *The Handbook of Social Psychology,* eds. Daniel T. Gilbert, Susan T. Fiske, and Lindzey Gardner (New York: McGraw Hill, 1998), 702–703.

6. Malcolm Gladwell, *The Tipping Point: How Little Things Can Make a Big Difference* (Boston: Little, Brown, 2000).

7. For a "biased scanning" theory of self-concept change, see Edward E. Jones, Frederick Rhodewalt, Steven Berglas, and James A. Skelton, "Effects of Strategic Self-Presentation on Subsequent Self-Esteem," *Journal of Personality and Social Psychology* 41, no. 3 (1981): 407–421. This line of research is reviewed in Baumeister, "The Self," 680–740.

8. Yale psychologist Daniel J. Levinson discusses the important role of "transitional figures" in *The Seasons of a Man's Life* (New York: Knopf, 1985).

9. Ibid., 91.

10. Anselm L. Strauss, *Mirrors and Masks: The Search for Identity* (London: Martin Robertson, 1977), 110–111.

11. Etienne Wenger, *Communities of Practice: Learning, Meaning, and Identity* (Cambridge, UK: Cambridge University Press, 1998); Jean Lave and Etienne Wenger, *Situated Learning: Legitimate Peripheral Participation* (Cambridge, UK: Cambridge University Press, 1991).

12. William Bridges, "Cool Friends," interview by Erik Hansen, 15 September 2000, <www.tompeters.com>. Reprinted by permission of tompeters.com. For more information, please visit the Web site.

13. For a recent review of socialization research, see Herminia Ibarra, "Provisional Selves: Experimenting with Image and Identity in Professional Adaptation," *Administrative Science Quarterly* 44, no. 4 (December 1999): 764–791. For a discussion of the need to make sense of surprising occurrences, see Meryl Reis Luis, "Surprise and Sense Making: What Newcomers Experience in Entering Unfamiliar Organizational Settings," *Administrative Science Quarterly* 25, no. 2 (1980): 226–251.

14. Erving Goffman, "The Nature of Deference and Demeanor," *American Anthropologist* 58, no. 3 (1956): 473–502.

15. Edgar H. Schein, "Kurt Lewin's Change Theory in the Field and in the Classroom: Notes Toward a Model of Managed Learning," *Systems Practice* 9, no. 1 (1996): 27–48.

16. John Bowlby, *A Secure Base: Parent-Child Attachment and Healthy Human Development* (New York, Basic Books, 1988).

17. Donald W. Winnicott, *Playing and Reality* (New York: Routledge, 1989).

18. John Bowlby, "Self-Reliance and Some Conditions That Promote It," in *Support, Innovation and Autonomy,* ed. R. H. Gosling (London: Tavistock, 1973), 23–48. Cited in William A. Kahn, "Secure Base Relationships at Work," in *The Career Is Dead—Long Live the Career: A Relational Approach to Careers,* ed. Douglas T. Hall (San Francisco: Jossey-Bass, 1996), 158–179.

seven

1. Karl E. Weick, *The Social Psychology of Organizing,* 2d ed. (New York: McGraw-Hill, 1979).

2. Dan P. McAdams, *The Stories We Live By: Personal Myths and the Making of the Self,* 1st ed. (New York: Guildford Publications, 1997), and *Power Intimacy and the Life Story: Personological Inquiries into Identity* (New York: Guildford Publications, 1988).

3. Charles B. Handy, *The Age of Unreason* (Boston: Harvard Business School Press, 1990).

4. Nicholson Baker, *The Size of Thoughts: Essays and Other Lumber* (New York: Random House, 1996), 4.

5. Joseph L. Badaracco, *Defining Moments: When Managers Must Choose between Right and Right* (Boston: Harvard Business School Press, 1997), 58–61.

6. Ellen J. Langer and Alison I. Piper, "The Prevention of Mindlessness," *Journal of Personality and Social Psychology* 53, no. 2 (1987): 280–287; Meryl Reis Louis and Robert Sutton, "Switching Cognitive Gears: From Habits of Mind to Active Thinking," *Human Relations* 44, no. 1 (1991): 55–76.

7. Kenneth J. Gergen, *Realities and Relationships: Soundings in Social Construction* (Cambridge, MA: Harvard University Press, 1997).

8. Baker, *The Size of Thoughts,* 7.

9. Edgar H. Schein, "Kurt Lewin's Change Theory in the Field and in the Classroom: Notes Toward a Model of Managed Learning." *Systems Practice* 9, no. 1 (1996): 27–48.

10. David A. Jopling, *Self-Knowledge and the Self* (New York: Routledge, 2000).

11. Manfred F. R. Kets de Vries, *The Leadership Mystique: A User's Manual for the Human Enterprise* (London: Financial Times/Prentice Hall, 2001), 182.

12. Arthur Koestler, *The Act of Creation* (London: Arkana, 1989), 113.

13. Ibid., 112.

14. Ibid., 108.

15. Teresa M. Amabile, *Creativity in Context: Update to the Social Psychology of Creativity* (Boulder, CO: Westview Press, 1996), 83.

16. In his work on leadership and corporate transformation, Harvard Kennedy School of Government professor Ronald Heifetz finds that successful change requires frenetic activity "on the dance floor" (such as crafting experiments, shifting connections) combined with a more distant observation and reflection from the "balcony above." Ronald A. Heifetz, *Leadership Without Easy Answers* (Cambridge, MA: Belknap Press of Harvard University Press, 1994).

17. Koestler, *The Act of Creation.*

18. According to a U.S. national poll conducted by Bruskin and Associates, close to seven out of ten people with incomes of more than $40,000 per year fantasize about taking a few months off, and one out of five thirty-five- to thirty-nine-year-olds fantasize about it daily. Reported in Hope Dlugozima, James Scott, and David Sharp, *Six Months Off: How to Plan, Negotiate, and Take the Break You Need without Burning Bridges or Going Broke* (New York: Henry Holt, 1996), 2.

19. Nancy Staudenmayer, Marcie J. Tyre, and Leslie Perlow, "Time to Change: Temporal Shifts as Enablers of Organizational Change," *Organizational Science,* forthcoming (fall 2002).

20. Marcie J. Tyre and Wanda Orlikowski, "Windows of Opportunity," *Organization Science* 5, no. 1 (1994); Connie J. G. Gersick, "Making Time:

Predictable Transitions in Task Groups," *Academy of Management Journal* 32, no. 2 (1989): 274–309.

21. John J. Gabarro, *The Dynamics of Taking Charge* (Boston: Harvard Business School Press, 1986).

22. Daniel J. Levinson, *The Seasons of a Man's Life* (New York: Knopf, 1985).

23. Gergen, *Realities and Relationships.*

eight

1. Carl R. Rogers, *On Becoming a Person* (New York: Houghton Mifflin, 1961).

2. For recent business press accounts of these trends, see David Baker, "A Good Time to Step Back from the Old Routine," *Financial Times,* 19 November 2001; Alison Maitland, "Trouble for the Problem-Solvers," *Financial Times,* 9 November 2000; Carol Hymowitz, "Midlife Career Shift: Investment Banker Prefers a Pulpit," *Wall Street Journal,* 13 June 2001; and Astrid Wendlandt, "Making the Most of Mid-Life Melancholia," *Financial Times,* 24 November 2000.

3. Hope Dlugozima, James Scott, and David Sharp interviewed 200 working Americans who took between two months and two years off from work. See *Six Months Off: How to Plan, Negotiate, and Take the Break You Need without Burning Bridges or Going Broke* (New York: Henry Holt, 1996), 154.

4. Samuel D. Osherson, *Holding on and Letting Go: Men and Career Change at Midlife* (New York: Free Press, 1980).

5. Daniel J. Levinson, *The Seasons of a Man's Life* (New York: Knopf, 1985). See also Manfred Kets DeVries, *Struggling with the Demon: Perspectives on Individual and Organizational Irrationality* (Madison, CT: Psychosocial Press, 2001), 95–119.

6. Erik H. Erikson, "Identity and the Life Cycle," *Psychological Issues* 1, 59–100.

appendix

1. Classic studies include Edgar H. Schein, *Career Dynamics: Matching Individual and Organizational Needs* (Reading, MA: Addison-Wesley, 1978); George E. Vaillant, *Adaptation to Life* (New York: Little, Brown, 1977); Samuel D. Osherson, *Holding On and Letting Go: Men and Career Change at Midlife* (New York: Free Press, 1980); Roger L. Gould, *Transformations: Growth and Change in Adult Life* (New York: Simon & Schuster, 1979); Robert W. White, *Lives in Progress,* 2d ed. (New York: Holt, Rinehart and

Winston, 1966); and Douglas T. Hall, *Careers in Organizations: Individual Planning and Organizational Development* (Pacific Palisades, CA: Goodyear Publishing, 1976).

2. For exceptions, see Douglas T. Hall, "Breaking Career Routines: Mid-career Choice and Identity Development," in *Career Development in Organizations,* ed. Douglas T. Hall (San Francisco: Jossey-Bass, 1986); and Osherson, *Holding On and Letting Go.*

3. See, for example, Michael B. Arthur and Denise M. Rousseau, eds., *The Boundaryless Career: A New Employment Principle for a New Organizational Era* (New York: Oxford University Press, 2001); Michael B. Arthur, Kerr Inkson, and Judith K. Pringle, *The New Careers: Individual Action and Economic Change* (Thousand Oaks, CA: Sage Publications, 1999); Douglas T. Hall, ed., *The Career Is Dead Long Live the Career: A Relational Approach to Careers* (San Francisco: Jossey-Bass, 1996) and *Career Development in Organizations*; Charles B. Handy, *The Age of Unreason* (Boston: Harvard Business School Press, 1990) and *The Hungry Spirit: Beyond Capitalism: A Quest for Purpose in the Modern World* (New York: Arrow Books, 1998); Elizabeth P. McKenna, *When Work Does Not Work Anymore: Women, Work, and Identity* (New York: Dell Publishing, 1998).

4. On experiential learning, see for example David A. Kolb and Mark S. Plovnick, "The Experiential Learning Theory of Career Development," in *Organizational Careers: Some New Perspectives,* ed. John Van Maanen (New York: Wiley, 1976), 65–87. On identity as possibility, see Hazel Markus and Paula Nurius, "Possible Selves," *American Psychologist* 41, no. 9 (1986): 954–969.

5. Edgar H. Schein, "The Individual, the Organization, and the Career: A Conceptual Scheme," *Journal of Applied Behavioral Science* 7, no. 4 (1971): 401–426.

6. While most researchers would agree that our social selves change a lot and that basic personality does not, there remains much disagreement on the extent of identity change. Schein's work, for example, indicates that "career anchors" do not change much by midcareer, even in the face of dramatic external change. In his studies (see Edgar H. Schein, *Career Anchors: Discovering Your Real Values,* rev. ed. [San Diego, CA: University Associates, 1990]), he finds that major changes are the result of a work situation that no longer allows or rewards the dispositions, values, and preferences that brought the person there in the first place. A different school of thought, however, holds that changes in the individual himself or herself are equally important motives for career change. Researchers in this camp show that values and preferences can and do change as a result of an individual's own maturation and

personality development, reducing the "fit" in the old work situation (see for example Kolb and Plovnick, "The Experiential Learning Theory of Career Development"; and Osherson, *Holding On and Letting Go*).

7. See Karl E. Weick, *The Social Psychology of Organizing*, 2d ed. (New York: McGraw-Hill, 1979); John H. Yost, Michael J. Strube, and James R. Bailey, "The Construction of the Self: An Evolutionary View," *Current Psychology* 11, no. 2 (1992): 110–121.

8. Adam Bryant, "They're Rich (And You Are Not)," *Newsweek*, 5 July 1999, 34–41.

9. Hall defined midcareer as ages 35 to 50 for a person with a traditional, uninterrupted career, that is, someone starting work at age 21 and retiring at 65. He notes that for a person with an early start or an interrupted or delayed career, the middle could come at quite a different point. Hall, *Career Development in Organizations*, 125.

10. Schein, *Career Dynamics: Matching Individual and Organizational Needs*.

11. See Kathleen M. Eisenhardt, "Building Theories from Case Study Research," *Academy of Management Review* 14, no. 4 (1989): 532–550; and Barney G. Glaser and Anselm L. Strauss, *The Discovery of Grounded Theory: Strategies for Qualitative Research* (London: Wiedenfeld & Nicholson, 1967).

12. Robert I. Sutton, "Maintaining Norms about Expressed Emotions: The Case of Bill Collectors," *Administrative Science Quarterly* 36, no. 2 (1991): 245–268.

index

about the author

HERMINIA IBARRA is Professor of Organizational Behavior at INSEAD, an international business school located in Fontainebleau, France, where she teaches in the M.B.A. and executive programs. Prior to joining INSEAD in 2002, she was a member of the Harvard Business School faculty for thirteen years.

Ibarra has published numerous articles and chapters in leading scholarly and applied publications including the *Harvard Business Review, Administrative Science Quarterly, Academy of Management Review, Academy of Management Journal,* and *Social Psychology Quarterly*. She has also taught in many corporate executive programs and given seminars around the world on human resources, career development, and organizational change.

She received her M.A. and Ph.D. from Yale University, where she was a National Science Fellow, and her B.A. from the University of Miami.